Dancing Before Azathoth

Dancing Before Azathoth
Macabre and Fantastic Poetry

Darrell Schweitzer

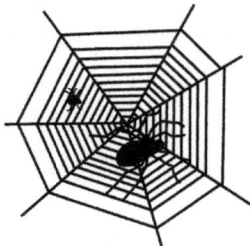

Hippocampus Press

New York

Published by Hippocampus Press
P.O. Box 641, New York, NY 10156
www.hippocampuspress.com

Hippocampus Press logo designed by Anastasia Damianakos.
Cover by Jason Van Hollander.

First Edition
1 3 5 7 9 8 6 4 2

ISBN 978-1-61498-478-8 paperback
ISBN 978-1-61498-490-0 ebook

Contents

Dedication: Once again, for John Sevcik,
this time in memoriam.

INTRODUCTION

There are some writers who do one thing exceptionally well. There are other writers who do many things exceptionally well. Darrell Schweitzer is without doubt one of the latter.

He has written fiction, poetry, essays, reviews, and treatises. He has compiled anthologies of fiction and nonfiction. He has conducted dozens of interviews of some of the leading figures in contemporary imaginative fiction. There seems scarcely any branch of literature that Schweitzer has *not* excelled in.

But his poetry is perhaps the most little-known aspect of his work, even though his first published poem appeared more than half a century ago and he has previously issued several volumes of his verse. This new book, containing work published in the past two decades, both encapsulates the diversity of his output and reflects some relatively new interests that have lately led him to produce some of his most vivid poetic work.

The very structure of this book reflects the broad scope of Schweitzer's poetry. In this regard it mirrors other aspects of his oeuvre, which ranges from pure fantasy to supernatural horror to psychological terror to historical fantasy to science fiction. In Part One, Schweitzer demonstrates how such traditional weird motifs as the ghost, the werewolf, and the haunted house can still engender a shudder in skillful hands. It is also here that we find several poems inspired by H. P. Lovecraft. That writer's signature theme of cosmic terror is reflected in the title poem of this collection; but in "Look Beyond" we find the same theme expressed in a non-Lovecraftian idiom.

In Part Two, we come upon the results of Schweitzer's relatively recent absorption of the poetry of Homer. He has always been interested in history, and his earlier work shows many traces of that interest. But (as he explains in the notes to this book) his reading of Robert Fitzgerald's translation of the *Odyssey* has engendered a remarkable effusion of poetry in which Odysseus, Penelope, and other figures in that great epic—as well as its companion, the *Iliad*—are brought to vivid life. Some of these poems may be only marginally weird, but they evoke the remoteness and compelling fascination of the ancient world in a manner that few writers today have managed. In other poems Schweitzer's reach extends to the realms of ancient Rome, the medieval period, revolutionary France, and all the way up to World War I.

In Part Three, Schweitzer looks to both the future and the past—the future as expounded by science and science fiction, but with nods to the space opera and "scientifiction" of a century or more ago. It is here that he engages in some pensive reflections on the fate of humanity as we wrestle with our technology-choked present and the prospect of our ultimate dissolution as a species.

Darrell Schweitzer has chosen to write most of his poems in free verse—but he has learned the valuable lesson that abandoning formal meter and rhyme makes the task of writing vibrant, evocative poetry harder, not easier. He knows that it is his word choice, his use of metaphors and symbols, and his ability to craft a poem so that it leads inevitably from beginning to end that will be the determinants of his success as a poet. But, beyond these technical skills, it is his humanity—his awareness of the fragility of our species in a world we will never fully understand—that infuses his verse with a poignancy and terror that every sensitive reader can feel. And it is this quality that will make his poetry endure.

—S. T. JOSHI

Seattle, Washington

PART ONE:
SPECTRAL NOTIONS

Dancing Before Azathoth

Came the demon
into the darkness of my dream.
Spake the demon,
"Rise up, take my hand,
and I will show thee
terrors never before imagined,
wonders never described,
secrets never written,
even in the blasphemous tomes of the mad."
So we plunged together into that place
beyond the confines of the grave,
where flesh and bones are sloughed off
and the spirit breaks free to soar.
We waded, stars splashing
about our ankles like foam,
and we dove down to where stone-faced gods
slept and dreamed and waited.
How we fled in terror
from the opening of their eyes!
All stars, all worlds, all dust of creation,
the very tombs of the gods
seemed no more than scum
on the surface of a greater sea,
through which we plummeted now,
in helpless fascination and despair,
until we circled and danced before
the black throne of Azathoth.
From this dream
neither my prideful, foolish demon,
nor my likewise foolish self

can ever dare awaken,
lest the lord of that black throne should rise up
and follow us back into the waking world
and devour it all.

Not All of Them Are Ghosts

Not all the voices you hear in the night
are necessarily ghosts.

The long, mournful howling,
that goes "o—o—o" without any message
might be an amorous owl, but more likely
it's the wind blowing over a pipe.

The voice that says exactly what you said
in perfect agreement, even as it fades,
is an echo.

The harping, hectoring, jabbering
that criticizes every detail of your life
and screams for you to do outrageous things
is inside your head.
You're having a psychotic break.

But the voices that strain to be heard
like someone buried alive, clawing for air and light,
the ones that ask you only to weep
as they plead for you to tell their stories
recall their faces, remember their loves and sorrows,
the ones that only under the most extraordinary circumstances
demand revenge,

those might be ghosts.

The Mysteries of the Worm

You who would learn the mysteries of the Worm
must first enter into the kingdom of the Worm,
waiting in that narrow house
until all flesh is stripped away,
all putrid organs devoured,
and even bones are left
rotting in the damp and the dark.

Then, assuming no demons or angels await
to carry you off,
you sink down through the world
like a stone dropped through pond scum
to grovel before the Worm King on his throne.

Perhaps you will become wise.

To climb back out
of that abyss
is a rare thing indeed.
Few try.
Fewer still succeed.

Those are the ones we fear.

The Poetry of Evil Must Never Be Shouted

Keep in mind that all the fun stuff,
the screaming virgin on the altar at midnight,
the swirling demons conjured out of the air,
and, most especially, the endless orgies amid standing stones,
are mere show-biz for the weak-minded,
not much different from the incense and mummeries
used to fill a collection plate.
Real evil is much more subtle,
its poetry never to be shouted,
its negation like a stain
left behind by oily smoke.
It has to get behind the eyes,
penetrate the brain slowly until
you face the abyss absolutely, and feel nothing.
Only then are you ready to reach for the knife.

Romance

Ah, the moon! The brilliant sky
at midnight as bright as day, the landscape
revealed in exquisite detail for miles and miles,
rolling hills, white farmhouses gleaming,
trees swaying in the gentle breeze,
a brook like a band of silver, and here,
up close, swans asleep on a pond like cotton puffs
on a perfect, dark mirror.
I remember the overwhelming scent of honeysuckle,
and how we two climbed, giggling like naughty children,
through a wooden fence, and stumbled, and knocked
it down; and we laughed at that too until we came
to a secret place and stood in awed silence before
a blank-eyed, stone god covered with vines.

You were already dead by then,
and had been for some time,
and I had grown so fat and stiff.
I'd blundered through that fence like an arthritic ox;
yet you whispered such things to me that I could only wish
that it were some delightful dream that would go on forever.
Only it wasn't.
Your hand was so cold it burned.
I still have the scar.

Dancing Before Azathoth

The Promise

When I have risen from the dead,
I'll build my tower on the plain
where no stone on another stands,
and summon back out of the dark
spirits that I still command
and demons that I once sent forth
to fight strange wars amid the stars.

Then I shall welcome at my door
such colleagues as still walk the earth
or, hearing of my return, have come
from grave or mound or ash-strewn pit,
to read aloud from arcane books
and chant as one the solemn chant
to wake the old gods from their sleep.

Still, I'll find the quiet hours
to feel the gentle touch of hands
and hear the voices I have dreamed,
and view, while lying in my bed,
faces bright as risen moons,
and know once more my loves and lusts
and all my sins I'll sin again.

Look Beyond

When first you gaze into the sorcerer's glass
you see only yourself, a reflection:
the innocent or fool or wise one,
eyes wide with expectation or terror,
face unlined or deeply scarred.
The details don't matter.
Look beyond.
Now the wondrous realms appear,
the crystalline mountains, the forests and fields made all of light,
the dark towers on lonely hilltops,
the wide, gleaming rivers that drift off to nowhere
beneath a brilliant moon, over the edge of the world,
into space and stars and dreams.
Look beyond.

The monsters rear up, ravening with delight
at the destruction of worlds, their gaze
locked with yours as if in a hideous dance.
This too will pass. It is vanity, a trivial game
of curses and dreadful runes.
Look beyond
into the real abyss, the all-devouring void
without magic or gods,
the utter annihilation of morality and volition.
Look at the shadow cast by nothing.
This is where it begins; this is
the first step of your pilgrimage.

Specter, You Have Nothing to Say to Me

Specter, you have nothing to say to me.
From the look of you, you're old, old,
and whatever happened, however you died,
my folks didn't even reach these shores
until at least a century later.

Specter, I see in your face
no passion at all, no sorrow,
nor rage, nor wistful longing;
certainly no wisdom gained
from the awful secrets beyond the grave.

You're like the last wisp of smoke
fading after the fire has gone out.
Is that what it's like?
Is that all there is?
Specter, have you nothing to say to me?

Angry in His Grave

So we buried him,
angry in his grave,
our friend, rival, mentor, master,
for all he'd opened up to us
the glory and terror
of worlds beyond,
for all he made us what we are,
when you'd think we should have been grateful,
we stuffed him into his grave,
because the literally goddamned fool
had bartered away,
not his soul, not his blood,
not even our souls and blood,
but the most precious gift of all,
his own death;
and so he would have gone on forever
with his thunderings and his conjurations,
and dragged us on forever,
had we had not buried him like that,
and he lies there, cursing,
angry in his grave,
and we know that we can never rest.

Dancing Before Azathoth

Those That We Meet in Dark Country Lanes

Those that we meet in dark country lanes,
should not be mistaken for the little people,
for they are not always little
nor necessarily people.
They leave strange footprints:
Was that a fox, or a goat,
or even a small horse?
Or one of them?
They converse in barks, chirps, and whistles,
though, being neither fallen nor unfallen,
they know the speech of angels.
With music and liquors they make us mad
and lead us into the deep woods,
until, laughing and singing and deliriously afraid,
we come to the place where the earth opens up,
and the ancient rites begin.

Lavinia Whateley

When the thunder spoke
and the wind filled her
and the seed of other worlds
burned within her womb,
did she so intimately share
her sons' monstrous dreams,
as they shared those
of their father,
that even as her flesh
was finally devoured
she went on loving her boys
with more than a mother's love
forever and ever?

The Thing in the Box

The thing in the box
is old and dry and dead.
The thing in the box
just lying there
fills my mind with dread.
I hear it scratching in the night.
I hear it whisper—
that's not right—
a thing of bones and scraps and tatters
shouldn't taunt me in my dreams
until at last I raise the lid and know
that none of this has been a dream,
when behold I that ancient, huddled thing
—and hear it scream!

The Howling House

The Howling House! The Howling House!
We kids all knew of the Howling House!
There are ghosts, ghouls, and witches, the townspeople said,
and a thing in the cellar that's never quite dead,
plus a tentacled creature that stealthily broke
through nine iron locks, from a chest of stout oak;
there are shrieks in the night, and hideous curses,
sufficient to go on for many more verses.
The Howling House! The Howling House!
You don't want to go in the Howling House!

Then Billy and Jilly and Otto and Jane,
amazingly daring or else quite insane,
said, "Come on in with us, we twice double-dare,
and if there are spooks, we really don't care!
Don't be a chicken, it's gonna be fun!
Only a chicken would turn back and run!"

But I just stood there on the doorstep
and couldn't take one more step;
I heard their chatter and their laughter.
I heard the sounds that followed after,
and Billy and Jilly and Otto and Jane
simply were not seen again,
but if you hear that howling, sure,
there are four more voices than before.

Now We Are Joined

Now we are joined in the dance of death,
just like in that movie, *The Seventh Seal*,
hands together, somebody up front
actually clinging to the robe
of the tall guy with the scythe and hourglass,
the chill passing back through the rest
like negative electricity, all strength, all will
drained away as we weave
up and down the gray hills,
as insubstantial as a curtain of rain.
I try to think of the Stoic epitaph:
I was not, I was, I am not, I don't care.
But it's no good: from up ahead I hear sounds,
not the shrieks or crackling flames you'd expect,
but babbling voices, traffic noise, trashcans banged together,
the roar of some engine.
Does it go on forever, as an adventure,
or is this where the horror begins?

Malice Must Dwell Within Your Heart

Whatever you conjure out of the midnight air,
whatever you summon from a corrupted grave,
for the sake of portentous prophecies,
is just shadow and a fading echo
unless malice dwells within your heart.

No witchcraft, no incantation, no tongue-twisting
recitation in a dead language,
no thousand pages of forbidden lore
can be anything more than pedantry,
unless malice dwells within your heart.

Let the flame of hatred burn pure and true.
Let it consume you beyond pleasure and pain.
Then shall your mummeries be as daggers.
Then can you call down death and doom,
As long as malice dwells within your heart.

Only in Dreams

Only in dreams can I cross that plain,
and leave my tracks in trackless dust
of burnt-out suns, and climb those hills
that guard the furthest, deep abyss,
where dead gods and fallen angels lie.

Only in dreams can I slip through time,
into the forbidden yesterday,
converse with crouching demons in
rough-hewn tombs already old
before the Pyramids were young,
and learn such lore that in Atlantis once
a wizard spake to a fear-filled king.

Only in dreams may I trespass
beyond the veil of my own death
and read my words upon a page,
like ancient runes on parchment writ,
and laugh at the mix of terrible truth,
well stirred with prophecy, nonsense, and dooms.

I know that I must live in dreams,
embrace the madness of the moon,
and in my mind forever shun
the murderous reason of the sun.

Giants in the Earth

The Bible says there were giants in the earth in those days.
It's true.
There still are,
only they're much older than the Bible or mankind.
Sometimes you can see their shapes
in the contours of the hills,
in the bare stone faces of cliffs,
particularly at sunset or in shadow:
swarming schools of monsters,
sounding and breaching like whales
amid million-year dreams
in which a hundred centuries are as a second,
and their slightest turnings or sighs
are only measurable in geological time.

Pray that they remain so:
If they should ever awaken,
they will surely brush us away
like vermin off a dirty bedsheet.
Pray that their sleep is long.

The Sorcerer in His Tower
Contemplating Possible Success

You don't suppose I've actually done it?
Could it be that the years of privation,
poring over arcane texts in impossible languages,
the gesticulating and other theatrics,
the secret formulae whispered into the air,
the rituals of blood and pain,
have summoned from out of the surly, sullen dark
something that whirls around me,
rattling the bottles on the shelves,
turning the pages of my great book,
then settling at my feet like some submissive dog
until I command it to reveal the secrets
of the fantastic worlds beyond time and the grave?
Either that, or this room is just drafty.
But I cannot lie to myself.
Even when there is no wind,
even when all lights are extinguished,
even in utter stillness and silence,
I know that I am not alone, that
I shall never be alone again.
You don't suppose . . . ?

We Who Have Encountered Monsters

What kind of survivors shall we become,
we who have encountered monsters,
escaped them, slain them, or come away
bearing monsters within us?
We know where the dark doors are.
We speak fluently the language of death.
We are past shame or hoping for pity.
The most picturesquely mutilated among us
have done their time as sideshow freaks.
We flaunt our scars proudly, ready to offend
because we know how very special we are.
We have, caged within our hearts,
that which yearns for havoc
and waits patiently for inevitable release.
Is this how it ends, then?
Do we become the monsters ourselves
and exist to terrify some new generation of victims?

How Witches and Warlocks Do It

Witches and warlocks can uproot a mandrake
and hear its shrill scream
without going mad, because
they are mad already, though
their madness is not of this world.

Witches and warlocks can swim in the earth
as in a dark pool, and grope
for the dead, then assemble their bones,
first to yield secrets,
and later to dance.

Witches and warlocks can cut out your heart
and put in a stone, so deftly, so subtly,
that you never suspect,
till one night they whisper
the name of your death.

Witches and warlocks have to be mad
to barter salvation for one moment's glimpse
of Satan's proud rage,
to embrace his despair
out of lust or revenge.

But that's how they do it.

Which Remained Untold

Harley Warren wasn't merely ripped to shreds by ghouls.
He descended to the very threshold of the Dreamlands,
where the solid, damp earth melted away like fog,
and he glimpsed those fabulous dream cities,
the moon-galleys,
and maybe even the dreadful light that glows
atop a black tower
in Kadath, in the Cold Waste—
but such wonders remained untold,
even as he tried to describe them,
because there were, unfortunately,
ghouls present.

Ballroom Dancing

That lady's dancing with a corpse.
See how she's placed her hand
behind his neck so his head won't roll.
Slow, slow, quick-quick,
then into the zigzag of the grapevine,
quick-quick-quick-quick.
Yeah, his footwork's lousy;
she flops him around like a stuffed dummy,
but a stuffed dummy with bones.
Quick-quick-quick-quick.
My God, she must be inhuman,
so strong, so cool, so perfectly graceful.
That other couple almost blunders into her,
and she just pulls away, smiling.
You'd think that if her partner had died
of a heart attack there in her arms,
she might discreetly maneuver him off the floor
to avoid a panic, but no,
that is not is what is going on at all.
She's clearly enjoying herself.
There they go, around the room again.
Left rock turn,
quick-quick- quick-quick- quick-quick —

Werewolf Poem

What fool or coward considers it a curse?
When Goddess Moon summons me,
I am not her slave; she sets me free
to roam, to ravage, to rend
the very night with my strong teeth
and my fierce voice.
She strikes off the chains
of propriety, morality, and conscience,
and bids me gorge on flesh
and sweet, sweet blood.
The ecstasy is indescribable.
I am exalted, raised up
beyond guilty, deceitful, wretched humanity
into the purity and innocence of the beast.

The Secret Pool

I know a place deep in the woods
where a black, crumbling crater sinks down
to a still, shining pool,
and there's a girl in it, long past dead,
her hair a clotted mass,
her face dissolving like some discarded vegetable.
I'm there too, not a reflection, but in the pool with her,
the two of us embracing like lovers
who have forgotten all joy, anger, lust, and passion,
the memory of our lives no more than the twinge
an amputee might feel from a phantom limb.
I stare for hours, until with the utmost effort
I am finally able to ascend from that particular Avernus,
clawing at the dank earth, craving the light.
Then I try to convince myself it was all a dream, nothing more,
until the compulsion overcomes me once again,
and I must descend for another look.

Only the Trees and Stones Remember

When I came again to my native place,
the streets were filled with jabbering strangers,
the houses and shops entirely transformed;
only the trees remembered, the ancient oak
under which I once sat and dreamed,
the beech I used to climb to perilous heights:
those were still the same,
and the stones too, in the shaded churchyard,
where the names were almost weathered away;
they bade me lie still among them,
among friends, foes, lovers, rivals,
for in the dust no passions stir
and all sins are forgotten.
But I could not linger; I could not stay,
as winds of guilt and conscience bore me off
to wander the world for centuries more,
until I came this way again
and only the trees and stones would remember.

Dancing Before Azathoth

Some Books Are Forbidden for Good Reason

Suppose I hold in my hands an infinite picture album,
in which you can never find the same page twice,
and each of the beautifully rendered, superbly detailed
scenes of strange cities or worlds,
or portraits, multifarious, enigmatic,
comes into existence when I turn over a leaf
and vanishes into oblivion when I turn another.
Suppose, as I very much suspect, this is also true
of the subjects depicted, created and destroyed
like passing shadows, as the pages must inevitably be turned.
Have I become a god, a master of life and death
for countless millions?
I can't keep it open to a single page forever.
What if I find a portrait of myself in that book,
and in panic or just carelessness snap it shut?
I wonder what became of the previous owner.

Fairy Song

Out of the darkness and out of the night!
We're coming, we're coming!
Bearing stout cudgels and knives of sharp flint!
We're coming, we're coming!
To snatch gold and silver and leave behind dust!
We're coming, we're coming!
Steal babe from the cradle in exchange for our own!
We're coming, we're coming!
To cut out your heart and put in a stone!
We're coming, we're coming!
You won't even scream until we are gone!
We're coming, we're coming!
We'll hide in your grave, make toys of your bones!
We're coming, we're coming!
All holes in the earth we claim as our home!
We're coming, we're coming!

Grave-Robbing 2.0: Intermediate

So why are we digging *him* up,
after it took so long to get him into the ground?
We thought he'd live forever,
infinitely powerful, evil, wise, learned,
always on to our conniving schemes,
who only let us go on living
out of some incomprehensible whim,
like a cat toying with wounded mice.
No, I won't shut up. Over the wall we go,
across the lawn in the moonlight, shovels rattling.
The last thing I'm worried about is the police.
Jail, an asylum, would seem like paradise.
Tell me again why we are doing this.
For ghoulish baubles? A talisman?
An intriguing ring with a finger still in it?
If he was buried with a book, it must be
a sodden mass by now.
If you're planning some kind of rite,
it may not be such a good idea.
Please reconsider.
The coffin lid splintered with surprising ease.
Now you've done it!
That shriveled, grinning face!
You snatch the coins off his eyes.
They're open!
Now you're consumed in raging flame,
without even time to scream,
while I go quietly mad.

Master, I serve you always, with love and loyalty,
though I admit I am very much afraid.

Patiently Waiting

That kitty, who sleeps by the fire,
may harbor a secret desire
to nibble the heart
or some other part
of the next person due to expire.

I Know There Are Giants under Our Hills

I know there are giants under our hills.
Their corpses shape the landscape,
their limbs beneath the long, rolling ridge lines,
their gaping skulls weathered into caves,
their bones gleaming in the chalk cliffs.

I know there are giants under our hills,
their slow and sombrous dreams transpiring
through root and branch in the dark forests
into a darker sky, until
we too are dreaming them.

I know there are giants under our hills,
eyes wide, staring into the darkness,
buried deep but filled with rage, waiting
until the trembling earth splits apart,
and they might rise for their revenge.

Our Ghosts Are Going Away

Our ghosts are going away,
thinning out the world
until there is no more magic in it.
No more lingering silhouettes on walls,
no fleeting faces in the windows
of haunted houses.
No more haunted houses for that matter,
just old rooms, the smell of dry wood,
creaking sounds that are merely the walls settling,
and shadows that are merely shadows.
Our ghosts are going away,
leaving us with silent graves,
dry bones, dust,
and the all-devouring void,
which inescapably awaits.

Dancing Before Azathoth

Bold Voyager

So the demon bore me up in my dream
beneath an ash-gray sky
and set me down on a beach of bare stone
beside a waveless sea.
I said, "I will cross that sea."
"No one ever has," the demon replied.
"Is it death then?"
"Oh, no," said the demon,
"The Styx is the most traveled of all waters,
and Lethe the most yearned for.
It is easy to reach both of those.
This is the Abyss, which has no farther shore,
where darkness yawns beyond the last extinct stars,
beyond the last rolling, black planets,
beyond even the throne of Azathoth,
and the void is utterly silent and truly infinite."
Nevertheless, I gathered such detritus as I found
along the water's edge, fashioned a craft,
and set out.
"Bold voyager," the demon whispered,
"Very soon you shall yearn for the Styx,
and thirst desperately for Lethe."

PART TWO:
MYTH, HISTORY, AND
OTHER PHANTASMS

Ithaca, Finally

Yes, the voyage was long.
Yes, he visited exotic ports,
Egyptian cities, Phoenician markets.
Yes, he acquired rare goods
and sat at the feet of sages.
Many were the summer sunrises,
many the winter evenings,
with a bit of piracy and rape on the side,
to keep the crew occupied.
He defied the Laestrygonians and the Cyclops.
He did not fear the wrath of Poseidon,
though he clearly should have,
and in the end he lost it all,
treasures dumped into the sea, ships sunk,
every last one of his faithful, greedy sailors
dead, wailing at him in the underworld.
When he got home at last, what did he,
a ragged and wretched wanderer
bring as a gift?
He made his son a murderer.
He spread desolation most generously.
He would have started another war
had not Zeus intervened.
In his return there was no happiness.
Better that the voyage had never ended.

Penelope, Sleepless

Who is this bloody stranger
who lies beside her at night?
Sure, he has washed, but
the stink of death will not leave him,
any more than it can be scrubbed
from the walls and floor of the hall
where he slaughtered the suitors.

He sleeps with his great bow
always within reach,
murmuring of battles,
or weeping for comrades lost,
or trembling in cold sweat
over something he must have seen
in the Underworld.

Of course their son adores him,
but does anything remain
of the man-boy who left her
nineteen years ago for the war?
She's losing hope,
certain that he is planning
another voyage.

Therefore, silently,
she gets up,
goes to her loom,
and resumes her weaving.

Odysseus in the Underworld
for the Second Time

At first they tried to rip his flesh
off his bones with their teeth,
his former shipmates, companions in war,
even the lordly Achilles,
but they couldn't,
because they had no teeth
and he had no flesh.
No offering of blood this time,
because his smoke-like hands
could not hold a libation dish.
He was as dead as the rest of them now.
"Better the slave of a slave on earth
than ruler here," they said. "We told you so."
"Nevertheless I *will* rule here," he replied,
and set off on yet another epic journey,
over the dry, cracked plains and ashen mountains,
through terrible silences,
until he actually reached the palace of King Hades
and found the gate open, the palace empty.
Perhaps Hades was away, abducting Persephone.
So Odysseus sat down on the very throne of Death,
gazed up at the black stars
that gleamed faintly in the dull gray sky,
and dangled his feet,
kicking the throne like an impatient child.
Nothing happened.
There was no one to command.
Silence.
Death's little joke had defeated him.

In the end he lay face down in the dust,
feeling no sensation at all,
while his companions whispered around him,
"We told you so."

Odysseus May Have Been a Scoundrel

Yes, Odysseus may have been a scoundrel,
a reckless captain who loaded himself down with loot,
raided innocent towns on the way home,
beguiled a witch, blinded the Cyclops,
braved Scylla and Charybdis
(taking a few casualties during each adventure),
until he had lost the entirety of
ships, crew, and treasure,
only to arrive in Ithaca a ragged wastrel
and sow a harvest of death.
By contrast,
Aeneas was a paragon of every virtue,
who carried his father on his back
out of the flames of Troy,
spurned the Carthaginian queen
when duty and destiny called him,
conquered foes and sired such progeny
as would one day rule
all the fairest parts of the world.
But which one seems vivid, a real man,
rather than a shadow,
alive, rather than a mere exemplar?
It isn't the unblemished hero.
I think the gods (not to mention the poets)
prefer tragedy, with a sprinkling of rascality
added for spice.
Suffering holds attention in a way
the exaltation of victory seldom does,
if only because we have all suffered,
we have all fallen short of our ideals,

and very few have ever been truly victorious.
If the end of life is the ending of life,
if even Rome, serene and glorious,
must wait for the barbarians,
then our only recompense is among the shades,
in the cold dust,
where all men are equal.

The Ghosts of Troy

Of course there were ghosts at Troy:
slain, defiled, dust-dragged Hector,
protesting uselessly into the wind,
and his foe, the vile and beautiful Achilles,
piercing the stormy nights with
screams and laughter to stop
the stoutest hearts;
not to mention the piteous murmurings
of the uncounted dead, the clangor of swords,
the cracking of limbs, the death-cries heard
long after the Greeks had sailed away.
The ghosts of Troy were as inevitable
as raindrops out of a darkening sky.

But the ghosts of Troy to be feared
were the ones that followed the victors home,
the same that brought Agamemnon
to a swift and degrading death
when he tried to reclaim his own bed;
the same that immersed Odysseus into such
an orgy of new carnage that it might have spawned
another epic had not Zeus, via thunderbolt,
declared that enough was enough.
Not one of the heroes lived out his days
in happiness and content.
Not one ever found peace.
The ghosts of Troy saw to that.

Homer Before the Trojan Court

Did the Trojan ghosts summon
Homer himself to perform before them?
Did Priam, Hecuba, Paris, Hector, Cassandra,
even little Astyanax hear him sing
of all they had lost?
Were they moved by the beautiful strains of the *Iliad*
to mourn for the countless, anonymous men
sent into the eternal dark because of
the relentless pride of heroes?
Or did they rage for revenge?
Did they cry out in pity for themselves,
or was that just the wind?
Did Homer, with hearing made more acute by his blindness,
realize that he was among the dead,
and did he, with greatest dignity,
without faltering once,
continue on to the end of the poem?

Was Helen there?
Did *she* weep?

The Gods Do Not Pity Us

The gods do not pity us because we know suffering and death.
They're jealous,
because we are truly alive and they are not,
because we can feel both sorrow and joy and they cannot,
because we embrace the world and taste all its flavors,
and they, mere abstractions nourished on sacrificial smoke,
cannot.

That is why they torment us and toy with us,
in an attempt to arouse those feelings they can never share,
and it is how we, when we live our short lives heroically,
or even hedonistically, defy them.
Because we can and they cannot.

Artemidoros, Descendant of Croesus

Artemidoros, younger son of a younger son
of a younger son of that same Lydian king
who was proverbial for his wealth,
having, ironically, fallen into poverty,
searched the wilds of Asia for his forebear's
fabulous treasure, discovering it at last
after searching ten years, or twenty,
or thirty (sources differ),
revealed by moonlight in the bottom of a chasm:
more gold, fine gems, and exquisite plate
than the eye could take in all at once.
Cautious and clever, this Artemidoros,
knowing that the king's wizards
would surely have set
some protection over such a hoard,
restrained himself, waited, and, sure enough,
just as the moon set, the chasm,
thundering, snapped shut
like an angry mouth or a miser's purse.
Therefore Artemidoros returned
the following night with an hourglass
and measured two and a half glasses
between the opening and closing.
On the third night he was ready.
He left his servant, Theon,
at the chasm's rim to turn the glass
and wave a torch when it was time to get out.
Then, descending, Artemidoros
walked in silent awe

amid riches beyond counting
and relished the sensual pleasure
of merely touching such beautiful things.
While he filled his sack he conversed
with the ghost of the old king,
who was neither angry nor proud nor mournful,
for the dead are beyond such concerns,
even if Croesus had managed
better than most of us
to take it with him.
The king, as ghosts will,
waxed philosophical, even long-winded,
with the bitter wisdom he had gained
beyond the end of life.
Artemidoros worked steadily,
selecting only the best of the best pickings.

Meanwhile the faithful Theon
turned the glass, once, twice, thrice,
and waved his torch frantically
for his master to return,
but to no avail, alas, because
Artemidoros, remote descendant of Croesus
and a chip off the old block,
never looked up.

Drowning the Sacred Chickens

(P. Claudius Pulcher at Drepana, 249 B.C.E.)

"Drink, then!"
With all the might for Rome
arrayed on the cusp of destiny,
perhaps because of the noise
or the heaving sea,
the sacred chickens would not eat,
the auspices could not be taken,
and the battle could not begin
until at last, exasperated,
shouting thus, the admiral
hurled their cage into the sea,
only to subsequently lose
the battle, his ships,
and every shred of his honor.
What did you expect?
It wasn't that the gods
were particularly offended by the blasphemy,
or that they were over-fond of chickens,
but simply that destiny
cannot be swayed or rushed
any more than you can hurl
rain back into the sky.

Sparta, in Decline

They do it for the tourists, nowadays.
In former times, boys were flogged
before the altar of the most holy goddess,
some of them to death, that the rest
might gain that forbearance and iron will
by which our city was so famously victorious.
Now fat Romans slump on wooden benches,
stuffing themselves with olives and candied meats,
or sipping wine, watching as they might watch
asses raping women in the arena,
or dwarfs set to battle against cripples
for a jaded emperor's delight.
Most of the boys are slaves.
They gain nothing but scars.

Yet in this place Lycurgus
once proclaimed the ancient laws.
From here King Leonidas marched
with his three hundred, grim
silent men in their red cloaks
and horsehair-crested helmets, led
to death and deathless fame
at Thermopylae.
Here, manly courage flowed
as freely as blood,
at war and preparing for war being
the only recognized states of existence.

I rage. I weep.
There are no Spartiates left,
        only helots.

The temples are shabby.
The houses are falling down.
The streets are full of mud.
Yet I tell you
that the heroes are still here.
Truly was it written:
Judge not Sparta by its architecture.
Judge it by its ghosts.

In the Roman Forum

(500 C.E.)

In the Roman Forum, bronze statues stand,
thick as trees in a German forest,
recalling the ancient and glorious past.
Every caesar is there, every princeling,
senator, prefect, conquering general,
and not a few imperial mistresses,
charioteers, acrobats, poets, clowns, and actors,
every *everybody* except that sanctimonious prig,
Cato the Censor, who said he'd rather men asked
why he didn't have a statue than why he did.
(Very witty, but no one's asking.)
It's entirely possible to imagine
that the sounds you hear on the wind at night,
the groanings, creakings, what might be muffled speech,
are the ghostly whispers of illustrious Romans,
reminiscing about the good old days, or decrying
the current, fallen state of things.
But let us not be naïve.
Those sounds are made by thieves
or by the Ostrogothic police,
who are in on the racket,
sawing through the ankles of the statues,
to cart them off one by one
and sell them for scrap.

What Shall We Do with
the Skull of Nicephoros the First?

(1014 C.E.)

So they've finally recovered it
after two centuries,
the infamous cup made out of the skull
of Nicephoros the First,
from which the inhuman Bulgars
forced our ambassadors to drink
to the everlasting shame of our Empire.

He wasn't a bad ruler,
this Nicephoros.
He greatly improved the condition
of the state, especially finances,
and even won a victory in the field,
before being suckered
into chasing the enemy
deep into the mountains,
where, amid sunless ravines,
they made short work of him.

Now our glorious Basil
has utterly crushed the Bulgarian army,
blinding the survivors,
sparing only one eye of one man in a hundred,
so he can lead the other ninety-nine home.
They say that when the Bulgar king Samuel
saw his soldiers returned to him thus,
he went mad and died.

So Nicephoros is avenged.

Dancing Before Azathoth

Should his skull then be laid to rest,
with solemn prayer and ceremony?
But look — that gold plating is *expensive*,
and, barbaric though it is,
the workmanship is *exquisite*.
The gems dazzle my eyes!
To the treasury, then.
Nicephoros was a treasury official
before he was emperor.
He'll understand.

Hadrian's Tomb

(The Castel Sant' Angelo, June 2009)

He isn't here,
that elegant colossus,
fool and wise man,
tyrant and philosopher-king,
impatient seeker
who tried to experience
all the world's mysteries,
everything this side of death,
and recreate it all in stone at his villa at Tivoli —
Here, in his final resting place,
he is merely absent.

For all we may imagine
this curving, sloping corridor
echoing with lamentations,
the air thick with incense and torch smoke,
the ancient priests solemnly placing
his ashes in the niche provided;
and though we may even be moved by this,
given to ruminations about transience of earthly glory,
it's not for his benefit,
because he is not here.

The ashes and the urn have long since disappeared,
either looted in the fifth century or hurled
onto the heads of besiegers in the sixth.
Later, someone thoughtfully set a plaque
engraved with his famous poem about his wandering soul
("Animula vagula blandula," etc.) into the empty space.

Up above: a papal fortress, rooms painted by Renaissance masters,
displays of Italian military uniforms that look like band costumes,
a very expensive restaurant, and an unparalleled view of the city,
not to mention a marble, sword-bearing angel
placed on the roof to commemorate an apparition
that appeared to Gregory the Great in 590.

But the emperor's ghost has long departed
like a flake of wind-borne ash, into the darkness
he wrote about and ultimately sought.

In Ghostly Ravenna

Holy Byzantium lingers here,
not as a fading echo but as a steady presence,
beneath starry heavens made
of wonderful, blue tiles, in the very rooms
and vaults the ancients knew.
Justinian and Theodora float like apparitions
in fields of gold above the altar in San Vitale.
We cannot help but feel
the shiver of their serene majesty
in the splendor of this place.
We're supposed to, of course,
but otherwise the show is not for us.
His portrait is from life, but she
was already dead and is surrounded
by subtle symbols of immortality.
Wide-eyed, the two of them gaze out from these walls,
not at us, but into another world.
We are no more than flies on a windowpane,
peering in on a mystery
we can never fully comprehend.

Dancing Before Azathoth

In the Ancient Lands

In the ancient lands
you get a sense of ants
crawling across cut stones.
Americans can't feel it —
not in their own country anyway.
A snaking mound or a mute flint
is just too remote, not enough.
But if you have seen Stonehenge,
or the piled rubble of the Parthenon,
or the layer cake of marble and brick that is Rome,
or the Chinese wall, or the Pyramids,
you think of those ants crawling on graves
or on pavement where Caesar walked,
or across a cathedral threshold:
something they didn't make, to which they can add nothing
except maybe a little hole and a circle of upturned dirt
from their digging between the stones.

I dreamed that the entire history of the Earth
was collected in a vast encyclopedia.
Heavy volumes lined the walls of some fantastic library.
Our story, that of mankind, was written
in a single paragraph on the last page
of the last volume.
In the ancient lands you can find
at least a few lines of that.

The Lost Dauphin Revisited

So now we know.
DNA testing has proven conclusively
that the son of Louis XVI died in 1795 while still a child,
his tubercular heart preserved in spirits ever since.
There were no unlikely escapes from revolutionary mobs,
no substitutions,
no fantastic travels,
no mystical encounters,
no tearful and amazing recognition-scenes.
Even poor, befuddled Eleazar,
who admitted that he might be mistaken
when he abdicated in favor of Louis Philippe,
was indeed mistaken,
and all the impostors were merely that.

The same is true of Anastasia,
murdered in that cellar room.
She wasn't Anna Anderson after all.
So our historical enigmas vanish,
like shadows when the light's switched on.
Just be glad the Iron Mask has never turned up,
and the song the Sirens sang
continues to defy analysis.

The Dauphin explained it all to me
the other night, appearing
not as the ragged, emaciated waif
he doubtless was toward the end,
but whole and sound and plainly clothed,
though faded, like a photocopy of a copy of a copy,
his voice no more than a whisper.

He said that survivals such as he
represent the deepest longings of mankind.
By such stories we defy death,
deny cruelty, embrace hope,
and leap toward eternity.
Therefore we should not regret his particular passing,
or Anastasia's (she was with him, holding his hand),
because there will always be more.
Someone else.
Always.
And then his words were not words at all,
but the breeze clacking the blind
as the sun came up.

They Believed in Fairies During World War I

They believed in fairies during World War I.
The first generation of young men
to grow up on Peter Pan
really did try to believe
amid scenes of unimaginable pain and horror,
and steal glimpses of beauty and impossible hope
on creased postcards and cheap prints
stained with the mud and blood
of Flanders or Gallipoli,
while the air about them swirled with lethal gas,
or stank of cordite and the unburied corpses
out in No Man's Land.
But none of them found their way into Fairyland.
The way there is long and hard.
If you try to walk the distance
True Thomas rode, you walk to your grave.
If you try to make your mind still
as a secret pool and wait
for Fairyland to rise up
like a bright bubble out of the mysterious depths,
you will likely be disappointed.
What you seek is a miracle,
and miracles, by their nature,
are arbitrary, which is why
Fairy Queens are noted,
not only for their exquisite,
unworldly beauty, but for
their haughty, heartless cruelty.

The Old Retainer's Tale

Death came to the wedding feast.
He came not as a guest,
but crept like a thief at the midnight hour
while in the smoke-filled hall
few of the warriors sat at their place,
or stared into their cups,
or played their games with bones and dice.
His tread was shadow-soft,
his face it gleamed, a naked skull.
It was by chance, I say,
and not by work of gods or fate,
that I confronted him
and took my faithful sword in hand,
and cried, "Come fight with me,
and spare both bride and noble lord."
But then the specter paused
and drew forth neither sharp sword nor axe,
nor any sharpened thing,
but touched my lip beneath my nose
and pressed, with dry, cold bone,
then laughed, this fiend, and softly spoke,
his voice like winter's wind:
"That place I touched you on the lip,
I've touched you once before.
Before each man is given birth
into the sunlit world,
I claim him thus and mark him so,
to fetch, when fancy strikes.
So it is that on this night,
your lord, who lies abed

shall there beget a mighty son
whom even Death might fear,
if touched I not, with a potter's touch,
his soft, unmolded clay."
Then it was I did my deed,
my only claim to fame,
for which I might earn passing praise
in story, song, or lay.
I struck the monster's head clean off.
It rattled on the floor.
I struck, and struck, and shattered bone.
My fellows held me fast.
"Old man, you're drunk," they said as one,
"You fight with empty air."
They hurried me outside the hall
and tossed me in the snow.
"Now sober up! And don't make noise!
And leave our lord to sleep!"
But one thing they could not see,
and none of them could know,
that I held Death's head in my lap
and held it firm and fast.
And through the night I, Old Blabbermouth,
regaled Lord Death with lies
and heaped up tales of mighty wars,
and riddles, boasts, and jests.
Distracted from his task he was;
I entertained him well
until first light of rosy dawn
and cock-crow drove him hence.

*   *   *

                                                Dancing Before Azathoth

Conceived that night within the hall,
with smooth, unmarked lip,
was our lord's son, a hero-child,
whom even Death might fear.

PART THREE:
PAST FUTURES AND
OTHER IMAGININGS

Monsters of the Stratosphere

It's been a long time
since any stalwart hero
wearing jodhpurs, flying cap, and goggles
landed a biplane on the Heaviside Layer,
as if in a cloudy field,
to battle tentacled, voracious fiends
from beyond the sky;
and the Moon these days,
in all its pits and hollows,
no longer harbors giant bugs.
Mars, cold, dry, almost airless, awaits,
quite free of thoats, Tharks, and rampaging Warhoons.

But the monsters are still there,
just lurking a little further out
into the eternal Dark,
their eyes agleam among the myriad stars,
like wolves beyond a campfire, waiting;
and the courage required to face them
is just the same.

The Steam-Man of the Prairies

He looks like an old stovepipe now,
or a crumbling chimney.
Birds nest inside his head;
the rim of his tall hat has long since
flaked away, his arms gone,
cavernous gaps in his shoulders
leaving his interior open to weeds and mice.

Once he was a ridiculous figure,
chuffing across the plains as he hauled
wagons, bales of buffalo hides, artillery,
some Great Sportsman's luggage,
a regular Steam-'n'-Fetchit,
Tom Swift's Mechanical Negro,
his own dreams ignored.

But Tom is gone now,
as are Frank Reade Jr. and the rest,
and soon his ruined body will be gone,
and his great spirit will leap forth
to run racing to the far, dark horizon,
to scatter the star-dust
as he climbs the bridge of Heaven.

Dancing Before Azathoth

At the End of Time

Dying at last
in a strange bed, perhaps
beneath a bloody red sun,
perhaps not (indoors,
he cannot see the sun;
shadows gather,
grays, silvery blue,
black),
the Time Traveler,
for so it will be convenient
to speak of him,
is left to expound
to no one in particular
on the recondite matter
of the dream from which he
has awakened, a half-opened door,
two faded white flowers,
day following night like the flapping
of a black wing, a name
he can barely remember but speaks aloud,
and the mystery of gratitude and tenderness
that lived on in the heart of man
once mind and strength had gone.

Did he have the answer?
He has not returned.
One cannot choose but wonder.

Amazing Stories Covers

If the future is
that imagined story-space
beyond our lifetimes,
something we will never reach
but which we can design and shape,
then I want:

a flying car in every garage,
personal jet-packs,
firm-jawed heroes in fishbowl helmets
battling monsters on other planets,
in the company of (if there is no objection)
nubile space-maidens in measuring-cup bras.

To realize this dream,
to make it the future,
all I must do is step aside
and make room for the galactic emperor,
his robot counsellors
on either side of his throne,
serene, wise, gleaming, and eternal,
and beyond them, a crystalline, spired city,
itself alive and ageless, capable
of replicating and resurrecting
its inhabitants again and again
for the next billion years.

Where Have the Space Heroes Gone?

Where have they gone,
the Gray Lensman, Captain Future,
John Carter of Mars, Northwest Smith, and Eric John Stark,
all those extraordinary, steely-eyed chaps,
bronzed by the suns and weathered by the winds
of alien worlds, with blaster or sword in hand,
fully a match for any cosmic terror
the outer dark cares to dish up?
Where have they gone?
Spaceships today seem to be populated
by the occasional blustering captain,
but mostly just interstellar working stiffs,
ordinary janes and joes, in for a long, dull haul
between nowhere and nothing.
Where have they gone, the heroes born
from the earliest dreams of the human race,
the kind Homer knew, the ones worthy to fight
alongside Gilgamesh, Beowulf, or Arthur,
the monster-slayers of the primal dawn?
The answer is: they're still out there,
deep in the black void, beyond the swirling stars,
beyond the reach of science, but waiting
for us to find them again, to bring them once more
back to life.

The Gods We Left Behind

The gods we left behind,
when mankind reached the stars,
were the little ones, the gentle ones,
the soft-footed gods tiptoeing in attics,
gods of hearth and cupboard,
of springs and wells and forest groves,
gods whose passage rustles dry leaves,
gods of obscure professions and obscurer origins,
whose very purpose has been forgotten.
Like the detritus of childhood,
we have swept them into a heap
and abandoned them where they lay.
But the gods do not lie still.
They fill the ancient Earth with voices,
like Prospero's magic isle,
whether laughing, mourning, or filled with wrath,
I really cannot say; I only know
that we have not heard the last of them yet.

The World's Ending Again in 2012

Oh, dear, the world's ending again.
Mayans this time. Their calendar
runs out in 2012, after which,
in the timeless void, it hardly matters
whether we are showered with stones or
eaten by jaguars; the end is the end
and the rest is silence,
except that the Amazing Randi once compiled
a helpful list of such prophecies to suggest
that the world ends in *most* years, or at least
often enough, dooms striking our troubled planet
with the regularity of waves lapping against a rock.
64 and 1000 C.E. hardly need mention.
As ever, Nostradamus stirs in his musty vault,
adaptable to any purpose; and we may gloss over
pyramids and pharaonic dooms, or the latest revisions
of Mother Shipton, and only shrug that Jeane Dixon
promised a cometary collision in the 1980s
and failed to deliver.
I have my own favorites, among them
William Miller, who got to do it *three* times,
twice in 1843 and once again in 1844, leading his flock
to sell their goods (why? what would they do with the
money?), put on ascension robes, and wait
for the City of God, like a freight elevator,
to descend and carry them to glory.
And I have to admire the chutzpah
of the Korean cult leader who invested the cash

in certificates that didn't come due
until *after* the appointed date.
Now that's what I call optimism.
So if the world's going to end in 2012,
I think we can pull through.
Let's talk about this again in 2013.

Tourists from Outer Space

Tourists from outer space
do not really experience our planet.
They rarely learn anything in Earth languages
beyond "How much does this cost?"
and "Where is the multi-species restroom?"
They hold their parties, their banquets,
their dances (if that's what those are)
by themselves. We do not mingle.
Even here, in our cities,
they live in their own worlds,
which they bring with them when they arrive
and take away when they depart.

When Time-Travelers from the Future Finally Reach Us

When time-travelers from the future finally reach us,
they won't come to learn our secrets,
because they already know them,
remembering what we have yet to experience.
We are they, after all, before we become
what they are.
It would make no more sense to interview an infant
about a life yet unlived.
Nor will they come to us to reveal
the end of our story in order to change it.
The laws governing such matters
surely preclude that.
No, I think that, knowing the end of our story,
which is their own story before it is over,
they will merely pause to wonder
at all we endured and all we did,
and gaze on us silently,
whether in awe or terror, I cannot say.

Very Long Conversations Between the Stars

(The Dreams of SETI Realized)

Suppose we really do begin to receive
radio messages from outer space,
zipping toward us at the speed of light.
It will be like opening someone else's mail.
A quick note from a cosmic next-door neighbor,
a mere two hundred lightyears away,
wasn't addressed to us, but to
James Madison and Napoleon Bonaparte.
Something from a bit further out might have been for
Ramses the Second or Hammurabi,
and, further still, kindest regards to *Homo erectus*
or even to T-Rex.
"How's the evolution coming? Hugs and kisses
from across a million years. Signed, E. T."
We could attempt to reply, politely,
"However much, dear friends, we might have wished
to share your cosmic wisdom, we shall all
be dead by the time you receive this, alas,"
or even "Return to Sender. Addressee Extinct."
In the end there is only one message
we can send to the galaxies:
"We were here.
This is what we did.
Goodbye."

Let Them Go

When the first true post-humans stand before us,
when, half machine, they stare back
with blank, metallic eyes,
or, perhaps discorporate,
seem no more than cloudy apparitions,
we can only let them go.
Hope that they will remember,
or even treasure, some part of what we were,
but let them go.
Let them fly off to the stars on gossamer wings
if that's what they have,
but we can only do what every parent must:
send them forth into the years we will never reach,
into the worlds we will never know.
Let them go.

Lacking an Adequate Metaphor
for the Human Brain

If it's not a computer,
into which our talents, memories, and very souls
can be scanned, uploaded, zipped, indexed,
then replicated onto a suitable backup;
and it's not a steam engine,
ready to burst with Freudian passions
unless the pressure is somehow released;
or even a fantastic cathedral,
a dream-edifice of cluttered rooms
into which mischievous aliens
sometimes sneak to rearrange the furniture;
or a closely written book where the turning pages
conceal but preserve all we have forgotten;
or paints stirred in a pot,
all colors and none;
and if the oracles and the very gods remain silent
and a hole in the skull won't let the evil spirits out,
then maybe, just maybe we're not
really sentient after all, no more
genuinely self-aware than a goldfish —
unless the goldfish,
floating, serene in his glass bowl,
knows everything,
but isn't telling.

The Mad Scientist's Assistant

I serve him out of love,
because he loves the grotesque,
and I, who am made hideous
by nature and driven forth from mankind
in a hail of spit and stones, am surely
grotesque enough to please
such a connoisseur as my master,
who loves me in return as we
rob graves and gallows and I stand
in worshipful awe in the crackling
glare of his exaltation, trembling
in the glory of it when I am allowed
the supreme honor of, with my own hands,
throwing some of the switches,
and the thing on the table begins to move.

Yet I torment the creature he has made,
that which, grotesque, should have been my brother,
because I am afraid that he will come to love it
more than he loves me.

Ten Reasons Not to Write a List Poem about the Meaning of Everything

1) Life, Man, God, the summation of human evolution, the far ends of time,
2) That's quite a lot to squeeze into a 10-part poem,
3) Even if I cheat a little bit,
4) Because once I've factored in Determinism vs. Free Will, Sts. Paul and Augustine, with a nod to the Fates, John Calvin, and B. F. Skinner,
5) I realize that this destiny may not even be mine.
6) The words just won't compress.
7) A better poet might bring it off.
8) Limited attention span.
9) Mathematically challenged.

Word Salad

So mix the words like a salad,
stir the nouns and heave the verbs into great heaps:
rocks, trees, horses, lampposts, sunsets,
blades, jewels, the moon, murder, love,
speak, run, build, wait,
chew, fornicate, wonder,
and sprinkle in a pinch of modifiers, prepositions,
articles, whatever else you've got:
Wherefore an aardvark?
Able was I ere I saw Elba.
Let the meaning come when it will,
should it deign to honor you with a visit.
Just pay attention to what is left behind:
The thunder of your dreams,
the hungry dark,
the bitter silence.

PART FOUR:
POEMS FROM EARLIER COLLECTIONS

He Unwraps Himself

He unwraps himself, like a Christmas package,
the ribboned clothing, the greeting-card hair,
nose and ears, nipples, penis, cast aside,
off —

He unfolds himself, with silent grace;
the face is next, a delicate mask,
lifted away to reveal
the skull beneath the skin;

Stealing phrases from John Webster —
Or was it Marlowe? One of
those leotarded guys — he unlocks himself,
declaiming, "Come, Sirrah! Gut me like a fish,
and give these groundlings
their sup of gore!"

Frenzied and fierce, he unbinds himself,
bloody sinews, lungs and heart,
the deeper flesh all steaming
at his feet, the gray-white skeleton
chattering in the dark, "But wait, my Love! There's more!"

At the very last, he reveals himself,
bones crinkled, heaped like newspaper,
the flickering candle's flame of his genuine self,
soul's truth, there, unadorned.
"Dearest, what you see is what you get."

*   *   *

But she hastily escapes through
shattered French windows,
and the night breeze
blows the candle out.

Each Evening Emily Dreamed of the Grave

Each evening Emily dreamed of the grave,
voiceless and trapped in the stiffling dark,
clinging to memories trickling away,
like sand in an hourglass, until she forgot
who she had been and whom she had loved,
tears and laughter, work and play,
bag and baggage of a life that is gone.

Even her name rattled away,
and this dream-corpse surrendered to a dream of her own:
the dawn's glaring light,
a stranger still asleep beside her,
and someone else's children in the hall,
shouting and clattering
on their way to breakfast.

All through the day,
amid chores, at meals,
pausing as she read a book,
or even as she made love,
she remembered her death,
and the touch of the grave.

"This must be resolved," her therapist told her.
"Wake up! Does the Chinese sage dream he has wings,
or does the butterfly dream it is a philosopher?
Wake up and see!"

And skeletal fingers shattered the coffin wood,
to claw their way upward through soft, muddy earth.

The Skeptics

Think of it as the plot
of a lost Greek comedy:
Gorgias, the stern philosopher,
doesn't believe in the gods.
and has raised his son, Philemon,
to doubt all things, save only
the head, heart, and hands of Man.

But on his deathbed
the old fellow gets religion,
while downstage the boy rages
that his dad's a sell-out,
a coward, hypocrite, and fool.

Then the gods appear,
invisible to Philemon,
but so numerous that they crowd the stage,
dazzling in their gaudy costumes,
whispering incomprehensibly among themselves
as Hades bears Gorgias off.

In the epilogue,
the philosopher's ghost tries to explain
that he hasn't been inconsistent.
He merely extended his doubt to include
the head, heart, and hands of Man,
which always fail in the end.

But Philemon can hear none of this,
raised as he was
to disbelieve in ghosts.

Dancing Before Azathoth

Heretical Gospel

Lazarus, resurrected,
locked in his shuttered room,
still stinks of the grave,
and knows to his bones
that nothing can render him clean.

For Lazarus, resurrected,
dreams of that soundless void
from which he was hauled,
like a fish on a hook,
into the thundering sunlight.

Now Lazarus, resurrected,
spends the whole of his time
in rapturous conversation,
with silent and unseen companions
speaking the speech of the dead.

Two Knights

The old knight rode through wood and waste
    before first light of day.
The young knight met him on a hill
    above the darkened bay.

The old knight spoke; his armor gleamed
    beneath the brilliant stars.
"Come ride with me, brave sir," he said,
    "and celebrate the wars—

"Crusades for Christ, my son has fought,
    throughout the pagan lands,
and relics of the Cross he's won,
    and held in trembling hands.

"A mighty ship, with banners bright,
    this morn on yonder shore
shall rest, and so my son comes home,
    to wander nevermore."

Then came they to the wooden bridge
    where living water flowed.
The old knight clattered straight across;
    the young drew rein and slowed.

"Come ride with me," the old knight said,
    "to welcome home my son.
Come praise his name; come praise his fame;
    come praise the deeds he's done."

The young knight sat in silence there
    in darkness on the hill.

His voice was like a cold, faint breeze,
    Quiet, rustling, still.

"I am the ghost of your dear son,
    in bloody battle slain.
I cannot cross the living stream,
    nor ride with you again.

"My coffin lies within the ship
    that anchors on the morrow.
Father, greet me there alone,
    in silence and in sorrow.

"And speak not of my battles won,
    my glory, or my worth,
for all the dead are equal when
    they lie beneath the earth.

"The rogue, the slave, the king, the lord,
    the wicked and the just—
What matter names or words or deeds,
    when all are clay and dust?"

The old knight rode to meet the ship,
    in silence and in sorrow.
He laid his son within a grave,
    and died upon the morrow.

Invocation

Mother Hecate! Mistress of Night!
Goddess of dread, of pain and of fright,
Goddess of graves, of death's holy fire,
Goddess of daggers, of hate and desire!

Come to the hanged man, who turns in the air.
Come as a wolf, as a hound, as a mare.
Come to the crossroads, with torch and with sword.
Come, as we call thee, come at our word!

We who would serve thee, offer up blood,
of black lamb and black dog, and infant new-born.
We who would love thee, offer our souls,
to murder and witchcraft, secretly sworn.

Goddess of darkness, bringer of woes!
Go from us after our covenant's made.
Make those who hunt us with good cause afraid —
Goddess of vengeance, visit our foes!

Dancing Before Azathoth

Not Your Typical Horror Poem

If this were your typical horror poem,
I'd have ripped your eyes out in the first two lines,
peeling back the skin of your cheeks,
so your grimacing redmask can sing along
while I play on your slippery bones
like some lunatic one-man band,
the new-slit mouth beneath your chin yammering,
as we two dance in mad embrace
all the way to Hell.

But this is not a typical horror poem,
so I'm not going to do those things to you.

At least not right away.

Concerning the Fate of Philip,
Emissary of Pope Alexander III to Prester John

This much might well be true,
that the pope wrote a letter,
dated September 22, 1177,
and entrusted his physician, Philip,
to deliver it, commanding him
to seek out the fabled domain
of John, Priest, Lord of the Four Indias,
most puissant Christian monarch of Asia,
and secure an alliance against the Saracens.

Philip never returned.
It is easy enough to imagine
that loyal and learned man
butchered by bandits,
or rotting in a dungeon far away,
or dying obscurely in some God-forsaken village
while strangers shook their heads sadly,
unable to comprehend a single word of his delirium,
and then placed the letter, unopened,
at the feet of a barbarous stone idol
until wind and rain and mice did the rest.
Or maybe the wastelands just swallowed him up.

No, I say.
We must demand more than that.
Let us insist, at least,
that brave Philip reached the wild marches of Asia,
encountering whole wandering herds
of seven-horned bulls,
and lions of red, green, black, and blue,

and griffins, which carry off oxen,
and Yllerion, which have wings like razors,
and, of course, unicorns.

Let us say, too,
that he crossed the Sea of Sand,
as Alexander did, carried aloft
by one of those griffins,
and came at last
to the river of precious stones,
and the land of shadow,
and the country of headless men,
whose eyes grow beneath their shoulders,
and other such marvels as are described
by numerous excellent authors.

I am certain that he beheld the Phoenix,
dying, burning, resurrected,
and I think that he secured a drop
of that holy oil
which bleeds from a dry tree,
a mere day's journey from the Earthly Paradise.

And I have dreamed that Philip was received kindly
at the court of Prester John
and allowed to rest,
while the pope's letter was read.

What then? He did not return.
Prester John's answer remains a mystery.
There are mysteries after all.
I merely insist on certain standards
so the trackless waste
won't swallow us all.

Signs and Portents

(Dinner conversation, Rome, 394 C.E.)

"The word has come from Egypt
  that the Apis Bull has appeared again,
  garlanded in all its expected magnificence,
  and that a voice thunders from the Serapeum,
  unintelligible but comforting nonetheless
  in its thoroughly traditional frightfulness.
  There's even talk of the Phoenix,
  and of a new age beginning,
  or a golden age returning.
  The Egyptian skies are filled with portents."

"The word has come from Aquilea
  that the truth-loving emperor Theodosius
  has utterly crushed the upstart Eugenius,
  and the murderer Arbogastes,
  and all their heathen cronies.
  There were the armies of Christ and Jupiter
  objectively weighed in the balance,
  and at the crucial moment a miraculous wind
  hurled the spears of the pagans
  back into their faces.
  The only voices that day crying
  were of the wicked, swiftly dying.
  At Aquilea, the skies are filled with angels."

"How very fortunate, then,
  that you and I
  aren't the sort to give credence
  to preposterous rumors,
  or to idle, wagging tongues."

Dancing Before Azathoth

The Sorcerer Contemplates His Beginnings

To think that once I was a child such as these,
a tumble of rags and dust in a village street,
or a trembling boy barely into his teens,
his heart thumping as he runs to meet
some sweetheart in the evening air.
The boy did not fear the darkness then,
nor ponder the mysteries of the Worm,
nor speak with thunder among the hills.
When did the fire begin to burn?

When he listened to whispers in the night
and learned that death is but a door;
when demons raised him to some height,
promising kingdoms, gold, and more;
when first he walked a shadowed path,
quite unknown to most mankind,
seduced by sigils of the heart,
and inscrutable hieroglyphs of the mind.

Then the fire began to burn,
and sorcery sparked to life within.

The Sorcerer to His Long-Lost Love

Come to me by moonlight
when the wind is in the trees,
and follow me in silence yet
and linger among these
fallen idols of lost gods
and fanes where wild thorns grow,
where once we walked and once we paused
a thousand years ago.

Now I conjure you amid
this city of the dead:
Rise from your grave by moonlight
before the night has fled,
and for an instant resurrect
the love we used to know,
when we two dwelt among these stones
a thousand years ago.

Nuclear Spring

"Now that the burning is over,
  Now that gray winter is past,
  Now that the pale sun beholds the earth through thinning haze:
  the naked soil
  and the wind-whistling wrecks of His cities;
  Now that Mankind is through," spoke the dog, shrieked the
      crow, said
  the snake and the elk and the cat—
"The secret's out:
  We've barked our last and cawed our last.
  We're done with pretend-animal noises.
  Now may we all speak the natural tongue,
  a congress of beasts,
  a parliament of fowls,
  with voices Man did not believe in,
  with words He could never hear."

"I plan to wax eloquent!" cried the crow, a soaring speck before
      he was gone.
"I'll shout dictionaries to the empty fields
  and tear the faces from scarecrows.
  Those are pearls that were his eyes—"
"And I," sighed the uncommon housecat,
  her hour come round at last,
"shall address whom I care to, as always."
"Me too!" said the fox.
"I've cooed my last coo!" the pigeon was pleased to announce.
  And the fierce bear unlocked his wordhoard,
  And the voice of the turtle was heard in the land.

*   *   *

"Humankind *lives!*" screeched the rat.
"I've met him in my travels;
  we scrounged for grubs together by the silent river,
  a sorry competitor, yes,
  but there he is!
  A few of him anyway."

"Say no more! Shut up quick!"
  And words became babble and cackles and yelps.
  Said the crow, circling back,
  "*Caw!* I need practice!
  We'll have to resume
  the whole damn charade."

Then rose the great whale
  out of the blackened deep,
  dying, the last of his kind,
  his island back volcanic with sores.
"Let mankind sing *my* song,
  that it may continue after I'm gone.
  The rest of you, go on speaking.
  Hide nothing.
  Join voices with his in our peaceable kingdom,
  without any master,
  without any judge,
  for Man is a beast now,
  merely one of us at last."

Dancing Before Azathoth

Cemetery Tour, Montreal,
Early November 2001

So we made our little jokes
and took our pictures
in the rain and the gathering dark,
as the mausoleums,
like cramped, windowless houses,
stood in sullen silhouette
against the yellow leaves
and the orange glow of the city sky.

Maybe we grew a little less jolly
with the realization that there was real pain here,
that the ones who had passed through these iron doors,
into these narrow houses, were still loved,
and even the pink lawn flamingos on one of the graves
didn't seem as funny anymore
as the dead waited patiently
for us to leave.

Death Is the Great Unwinding

Death is the great unwinding,
like a ball of string undone.
The relatives slip away from your grave
by ones and twos,
the sun breaks through the clouds,
and after a while you get up,
touch your wife's hand again,
and promise to love her forever.
Then you return your gold watch to the office
and sit down at your desk,
full of the experience and wisdom
of so many years on the job,
and take up your labors with real fervor,
forgetting everything as you blunder your way
down the corporate ladder
until they finally show you the door.
For the moment you are free as air,
the world is your oyster,
and the one you'd sworn to love
is just a name among many
until the schoolbell rings,
and unwillingly you drag yourself inside,
to forget so many lessons
in favor of cartoon shows
and games of shoot-the-man-down,
and getting your bottom paddled
for unremembered transgressions
that seemed so right at the time.
But even parental pigheadedness fades,

and you unremember in flashes now:
going into the darkened attic alone during a thunderstorm,
the musty, waxen smell of Great-Grandmother
when you were raised in her arms for a kiss,
and dumping a bowl of applesauce on your head
because you just had to do it,
and some impossible-to-retrieve dream
about boys in pajamas, running,
who had once been Indians with Peter Pan.
Then life doesn't come reeling back like a yo-yo.
There's nothing on the end of the string.
That's it, then.
That.

Witches in Winter

Those aren't crows,
the tiny specks that you see
just above the horizon
against the steely sky,
as the night comes on
and the dead cornstalks
rattle in the frigid wind.

Those aren't crows,
screeching, faint and far away,
as cattle die amid the barren fields,
and old people shiver by the fire,
certain they'll never see the spring,
as sick children cry out in delirium,
and shadows deepen and nightmares begin.

Those aren't crows.

Dancing Before Azathoth

Dreads

What if our wizards are long-winded frauds,
and poor Tom's just left a'cold,
and what if our specters are shadows and wind,
and half-garbled memories grown old?
And what, too, if there aren't any dragons,
nor gods on Olympus, nor ogre nor elf,
and a knight's quest ends with a Triple-A map,
and the Grail gathers dust on a shelf?

I say that we *need* our shambling beasts,
zombies and hundred-foot apes,
and tentacled things from out of the deep,
and vampires in dark opera capes.
How much braver to conquer them, then,
creating ourselves what we fear.
The point is not tilting at windmills,
but making the giants appear.

Those Who Do Not Find Their Way
into Elfland

Black Jack Davey danced into the gloaming;
Tam Lin fell from his horse in the darkening wood;
King Orfeo played his harp before a long, gray stone;
Tom O'Bedlam was there all along;
and True Thomas, most famous of them all,
waited beneath a tree
until the Fairy Queen herself
took him on her milk-white steed
for forty days and forty nights,
riding in red blood to the knee.

But those who would command
the wonder to appear
can pore over their maps,
blow their horns,
and gallop till they drop,
and what they will experience after that
will be, no doubt, only delirium.

The dream comes as the dream comes.
Seek it without seeking,
as True Thomas did, sitting still.
If you reach out and try to grab it,
Elfland will recede from you
as the tide over flat sand,
across a space that would weary the comet.

Dancing Before Azathoth

Edgar Allan Poe Nears His End

He was doomed by 1847,
with Virginia gone, transformed
by disease into an exquisite china doll.
Now art and life commingled
as he crept out silently,
secretly, to mourn his Annabel Lee
in her chilly tomb.
Oh, he put up a brave front,
a pretense of returning to life,
as he received guests courteously
and even outclassed several gentlemen
in the boyish spectacle of a jumping contest
in which he split his gaiters.

But those who diagnosed "brain fever,"
drawing on whatever quackeries or ill-wishes,
more or less had it right:
he was not long for this world,
for all his seeming vigor,
the resumption of literary slugfests,
and even his frantic, preposterous
outpourings of love to Annie Richmond,
Sarah Helen Whitman, and others,
as if he might actually find
in a *living* woman the Ideal he sought.
These things were masks, which had to come off,
as the festival ended, as inexorably he voyaged,
like the traveler gliding into Arnheim
(by way of Auber, Weir, and Usher)
toward the cataract, and the towering, shrouded

figure that Arthur Gordon Pym saw,
whose hue was of the perfect whiteness of snow.
There. *There.* In the abyss.
The impossible Mystery, the Hieroglyph.
His pain was unbearable then.

The Colossi of Memnon Near Thebes

(Second or Third Century C.E.)

Sometimes, on moonless nights,
when only the brilliant stars
gleam on the black Nile;
with the desert wind at their backs,
the great statues are heard to converse:

"I remember playing by the river's edge.
The mud was soft between my toes.
Women scolded me.
I was terribly afraid of crocodiles."

"I am a god.
My father is the thunder, my mother the dawn."

"I remember love and laughter upon the waters.
I played the flute beneath the bright moon.
I remember the heady smell of the ripe grain
and the songs of the boatmen."

"I have always been made of stone."

"That was later. Now, of course,
Caesars come to gaze on me and wonder.
Their ladies write Greek poems on my feet.
But I remember life and the pain of life's ending."

"I remember nothing.
I am as I have always been."

Then the sun rises,
and the slowly heated stone

expands along some hidden fault,
and the stones begin to hum,
then sing, without words,
without any thought or remembrance at all.
Truly, this is the speech of the gods.

Glastonbury, 1995

Of course it was beautiful,
almost beyond words,
the Tor by moonlight,
the ruined tower at the summit
like a giant's index finger
thrust into the velvet sky.
Yes, I felt the magic then.
Earlier that day, in the town,
we had visited the Chalice Well
and encountered an exotic survivor
of an ancient, lost world,
a genuine, psychedelically clad,
barefoot hippie, doubtless an American,
here for the vibes.
We laughed at the crystals
for sale in the shop windows,
and such authentic, Arthurian paraphernalia
as a gaudy, gilt Buddha.
But on the Tor, at moonrise,
as we wound our way slowly up
the steep path where so many thousands
had trod before us,
on one of those rare, clear nights
when the whole of southern England
is spread out before you in the darkness
beneath the brilliant stars,
I saw things very differently.
A small group had gathered in the tower.
Someone played upon that most characteristic
of Celtic instruments, the diggery-do,

and the sound was low and soft and somber,
like a wind summoned and tamed by Merlin.
Someone else danced, a quiet shuffle.
I could well believe, then,
that here amid the Summer Country
the Otherworld was very close,
and the hill beneath our feet
could, at any moment,
split open like a ripe fruit,
spewing forth dragons
and the hosts of awakened heroes,
resplendent in their shining armor
by silver moonlight.
Yes, I felt it then.

A Barbaric Song

Whet our swords for ravens' feasting!
Open wide the doors of Hell!
'Tis the dawn of ravens' feasting,
time of doom and omens fell!

Draw our swords for ravens' feasting!
Shields will split and skulls will crack!
Bring the noon of ravens' feasting!
Heroes strike, the skies turn black!

Sunset of the ravens' feasting!
Broken swords in bloody hands!
Heap the flesh for ravens' feasting!
Ghosts flee howling through the lands!

What If I Were Secretly the Phoenix?

What if I, dull, graying, and somewhat
overweight, were unknowingly
disguised in human form,
that fabulous firebird of Antiquity,
given to inconvenient self-combustion,
just as it has made itself
comfortable in a cluttered nest
filled with books, pulp magazines,
a stamp collection, a whole wall
of phonograph records,
plastic airplanes I've had since I
was a kid, not to mention a genuine
1962 vintage Aurora Model Kit Dracula
in perfect condition — complete
with the original bat! —
along with the fossil trilobite
I found in a quarry when I was nineteen,
and, yes, all those filing cabinets
filled with letters and photos,
manuscripts and memories,
the gradual accumulation of self
which takes a lifetime to achieve?
What if, yielding to a mysterious,
inner trigger I were suddenly transformed
into something more beautiful and terrible
than the eye can look upon?
Then it all goes up in smoke,
all that stuff, even the lovingly painted
Dracula with his bat, and,
alas, you too, my dear,

utterly destroyed
in my appalling embrace.

Here's the rub:
The Phoenix is reborn.
Everything else isn't.
I am sure I would search
for you, disconsolately
poking my finger
through the ashes,
but ashes remain ashes.
Nothing survives,
except possibly the trilobite.
The neighbors have
every right to call
the Fire Marshal.
What if I really am
the Phoenix?

I Think That We Are Witches Now

We have our little secrets, you and I,
riding to meet the Black Man on the moor,
signing our names in his terrible book,
cavorting naked at the Sabbat.

I think that we are witches now.

But these are antics for the young,
who still have the energy
for all that cavorting,
not to mention spells, notions, and potions.

I think that we are witches now.

When I married late, a teenager into my forties,
I knew life would be full of surprises
and little adjustments,
but I swear by Him Below
that when you led me onto the roof at midnight,
both of us in our pajamas,
I was the one who protested, hey,
we're middle-aged and respectable, and
what will the neighbors think?
But you only laughed and dropped off the edge,
backward, like a diver off a boat,
and I screamed, "No, don't!"
because I thought I'd lost you.
Then you laughed again, floating in the air,
your bathrobe flapping like a cloak.
You held out your hands,

Dancing Before Azathoth

and I took them
and stepped into the air.

I think that we are witches now.

Lying in the cardiac ward brings a certain maturity,
even if the nurses call me "the kid."
It changes one's perspective.
A threshold has been crossed.
I could use some notions and potions right away.
But still I wait for you to tell me
that we shall soar through the night,
with or without brooms,
and dance till dawn on some black mountaintop.
Tell me we can still do it, please.

I think that we are witches now.

A Further Voyage to Byzantium

So you come at last
to the holy city of Byzantium.
There are no golden birds singing in metal trees,
only muffled hoofbeats, shouts, and the occasional thwack
of boys playing a game like polo
in the grassy ruin of the Hippodrome,
their cries like crows, faint and far away,
at the end of a long summer's day.
You pass street after street of silent, roofless houses,
and cross fields where the pavement has been torn up
to plant crops, as if no city of Byzantium existed at all.
This is a place of ghosts, of memories,
of the echoes of great names no longer spoken aloud.
In Hagia Sophia, yes, you can still feel the shiver
of miracles from another age, and gaze up in amazement
at the glowing mosaics of saints and emperors,
caught in the last gleam of sunset,
strangers, like yourself, from out of the deeps of time.
Step back to see better. Plaster crunches underfoot.

Meanwhile, in Blachernai Palace,
the last, loyal guardian of the Ancient Word,
which descends upon holy Byzantium directly from Christ,
and somewhat more obscurely from Julius Caesar,
waits patiently for the end.
This is a city for old men,
at the precise moment when the dream
passes out of the body
and becomes truly and forever a dream.

Dancing Before Azathoth

They Sure Eat a Lot in Epics

They sure eat a lot in epics.
The Greek heroes seem to spend
more than half their time feasting,
all their comings and goings
celebrated for thousands of lines
about pigs or oxen slaughtered,
the hindquarters sacrificed to Zeus,
the rest gorged upon amid
whole oceans of alcoholic beverage —
a wine-dark sea indeed! —
with more than a few drops spilled out
in libation to the gods.

Homer's world must have been noted
for sticky floors, but not, I think,
for rising blood-pressure, diabetes,
or cirrhosis of the liver,
or even, with a few memorable exceptions,
gray beards.

There was no old age for Agamemnon,
murdered on his own doorstep
as he came home from the war.
Achilles, the James Dean of his day,
made the choice
to live fast and die young.
Odysseus' entire crew,
when they butchered the cattle of the Sun
and earned themselves a thunderbolt,
quite literally gave their lives
for one last outdoor barbecue.

More certainly than any philosophers,
those men knew how fleeting
are the things of this world,
how soon the taste of the wine
will fade into nothingness,
and the beef become as dust.
Therefore the epic hero
embraces the whole world
and shoves it into his mouth
as fast as possible
without concern for spreading waistlines
or the condition of his arteries.
His mouth and belly will be empty again,
soon enough, in the dark,
in the cold, among the shades.

I Dreamed That I Sailed in a Ship of Heroes

I dreamed that I sailed in a ship of heroes,
across a wine-dark sea as smooth as polished glass.
The wind bellied the sail,
but there was no strength in it.
So we rowed in silence
against the piercing cold
until we came to the shores of Death,
and there debarked on the bone-pale sand,
our bright armor gleaming,
shields clattering, swords drawn,
the horsehair crests of our helmets rippling
in that same impotent breeze.
We fought our way inland,
overwhelming Hades' legions, cutting them down like wheat,
their thick, stagnant blood offered in libation
to the Dark God and the Veiled Queen,
whose thrones proved empty when at last
we broke into the black palace at the center of Hell.
Then we all milled about
in confusion at the moment of victory,
until each man heard a familiar voice
or felt a gentle, remembered touch,
which led him away into the darkness.

I found my father there in the Underworld.
He sat in the same hospital bed where I'd seen him,
on the last day when he was alive,
in a sunny hospital room in Florida.
He was in good cheer and full of stories,
but in a reflective moment he reminded me

that elders, particularly parents,
are our last line of defense,
and when they're gone
it is each of us who stands unprotected
in the front line of a battle no one can win.
"Dad, did you fall in the struggle?" I asked.
He replied, "No, I struggled in the fall."
And as I struggled to figure that one out,
I awoke to the sound of the alarm-clock ticking
and the wind fluttering calendar pages.

Sir Boss Remembered

(By the Survivors of
A Connecticut Yankee in King Arthur's Court)

CLARENCE:
We few, we proud and select few,
we vanishing few,
burdened by his confidences,
his industry, his gimcracks—
To think that we served him with such zeal!

THE COMMONS OF ENGLAND:
The Fiend! The Fiend! The very Devil incarnate!

CLARENCE:
He slaughtered countless thousands out of spite,
in what he described as a short and boring interval.
I think that he had become as unfeeling
as the steel armor he would not deign to wear.

THE COMMONS:
The serpent sent among us!

SANDY:
No, I think he could still love.
I think loved me for a time,
and that love nearly redeemed him.

CLARENCE:
Nearly is not good enough.
If he taught me anything, it was precision,
that exasperated mechanic who smashed all he'd built
because it did not please him,
and didn't give a God-damn about the rest of us,

that monstrous drillmaster who said, "These dolts will
never march lockstep, as proper cogs in my machine, so
to Hell with them all."
And to Hell he sent us.

SANDY:
I saw tenderness in his eyes
when our child was ill.

CLARENCE:
Or was it mere possessiveness,
the fear that something that was his
might be taken from him?

SANDY:
I wept for him.

CLARENCE:
So too did Attila the Hun's wife weep for him,
most extravagantly, as is written in a book —

SANDY:
That is nothing to me.

CLARENCE:
Because he didn't teach you to read, did he,
any more than he taught his horse or his dog,
or anything else he already owned?

SANDY:
I saw goodness in him.

CLARENCE:
I'll tell you what I saw.
I saw Satan trying to be God,

like a child too small to fill his father's shoes,
and so he picks up one of those shoes
and smashes everything in sight.
I saw it all in one, terrifying instant,
at the tourney, when things got serious at last,
and with six-guns blazing he neatly potted
near a dozen knights.
I saw it in his eyes,
no regret that he'd had to do such a thing,
nor anger, nor even the legitimate triumph of victory,
but the malicious, unholy glee
of the small child who has smashed what there is to smash,
and now hefts his father's shoe in his hands
like a favorite toy. He was truly happy then,
in that instant, as he sinned the sin of Cain.

SANDY:
Nevertheless, I mourned for him.

CLARENCE:
Death take me! I can't get it out of my mind!
In the end I became a monk
for the healing of my soul,
orphaned like all the rest,
with nothing to do but bury the countless dead,
unable to find any comfort for the living
and certain of my own damnation,
because I had found playing his game
and building his horrible engines
so much fun.

COMMONS:
The Fiend! God save us from the return of such a one!

Remembering the Future

We remember the future,
the bright, curving horizons gleaming
on viewscreens against a backdrop of stars,
space-armored legions clanking
past rows of hulking machines
like enormous vacuum tubes
to confront the all-metal worlds:
planets armed and powered
as only planets can be,
and dropped out of hyperspace
like so many ping-pong balls.
We know that mankind will triumph
in the end, even as we know
that Mars with its blown-glass cities
and Venus with swamps and dinosaurs
are out there, waiting.
We are, after all, the race
that will rule the Sevagram,
whatever that is.

But time passes.
The future fades.
We look back on it fondly,
yet with little conviction.
How very selfish to think
it was ever ours alone.
No, once you and I
have long since been absorbed
into the Cosmic Overmind,

or are just specks of dust
in a Lensman's wake,
the future will remain.
Let us remember it fondly, then,
in great detail
and pass it on,
like the treasure that it is,
to our children.

Scientific Romance

When we were master and mistress of the world,
when our airships soared like apocalyptic visions
above the helpless navies,
we could have erased whole cities,
even continents, at the touch of a lever,
with our bombs, gas, and radium rays,
forcing mankind to yield to our demands.
But, lacking any messianic agenda
or the desire to slaughter anonymous strangers,
we merely voyaged on, admiring
the Alps and Himalayas gleaming like icy teeth,
and the brilliant moonlight on the clouds below.
I steered the great vessel; you held my hand steady
while kings and kaisers trembled
at the thunder of our engines.
In the end we dismissed all our minions
on good pensions, detonated the secret island base,
and in our old age sat side by side
on cold winter's nights,
feeding plans and blueprints into the fire,
reminiscing about the times we had,
very much aware of what might happen
if such knowledge ever fell into irresponsible hands.

NOTES

Archibald MacLeish told us that a poem should not mean but be, and the poem "Word Salad" suggests as much. So is it worthwhile to comment further in a collection like this?

Sometimes.

The ghostly poems are pretty much ghostly poems and require little exposition. I assume most readers who have gotten this far know who Lavinia Whateley is. If not, run, do not walk to the nearest bookstore (or your bookshelf) and read "The Dunwich Horror" by H. P. Lovecraft.

"The Howling House" is an attempt to write in the manner of the late great Stanley McNail, whose Arkham House collection *Something Breathing* is a gem. Did I succeed? No, but I think the result is entertaining.

"Which Remained Untold" alludes to events in Lovecraft's "The Statement of Randolph Carter." But you probably knew that.

The dance-steps in "Ballroom Dancing" are elementary foxtrot. I actually had dance lessons until my wife concluded that I was singularly untalented in this endeavor. I do not know that anyone thought it was like dancing with a corpse; more like wrestling with a barrel.

"Fairy Song," I imagine, is sung (or hissed) by the sinister Little People of Arthur Machen's fiction, or Robert E. Howard's "Worms of the Earth."

"Patiently Waiting." Why is there *just one* limerick in this book, when I have achieved a certain notoriety with the form? The answer is too obvious. When I was compiling *The Pratfall of*

Cthulhu in 2019, that volume was intended to be a catch-all for such things, but somehow I missed this one, and a darkly sinister cat limerick is just too precious to waste.

The historical and mythological poems may benefit from a bit more explanation. I was bowled over by Homer's *Odyssey* when I finally found a version I could read (Robert Fitzgerald's) rather later in life than I should have. I initially joked that I was surprised that any of the Simpsons could write that well, but my serious obsession has always been with the ending, in which Odysseus comes home, perhaps wracked with guilt, perhaps somehow wise, but he then covers himself in blood, killing all the suitors, rather than just announcing himself and saying, "Okay, guys, party's over. Do not steal the silverware on the way out." This merely shows how far we are from the mentality of Homer's audience. We are not they. We cannot possibly understand, at the deepest level.

"Ithaca, Finally" is a humble reply to a similarly entitled poem by the great twentieth-century Greek poet C. P. Cavafy, the author of "Waiting for the Barbarians." Discover him if you have not.

"Artemidoros, Descendant of Croesus." You may search in vain for this story in your mythological reference books. I made it up.

"Drowning the Sacred Chickens" purportedly happened as described, during the First Punic War. The Roman fleet came around the southern coast of Sicily, then up the western side. They caught the Carthaginians in harbor. But custom required that the auspices be taken to know the will of the gods before the battle could begin. There were "technical difficulties," and the Roman fleet sat there for a couple of hours, while the Carthaginians deployed and pinned the Romans against the shoreline. To everyone's embarrassment, Pulcher survived.

"Sparta, in Decline." Back in the good old days of Sparta's glory, Spartan boys in training were flogged once a year, to toughen them. It is only a small stretch of the imagination that this became a tourist attraction in Roman times.

"In the Roman Forum." A perfect metaphor for departed glory, I think. The Forum is still filled with the pedestals of missing statues. Bronze was a valuable scrap metal back then, so much so that the only reason the bronze doors of the Pantheon were not carted off and recycled is that they weigh a ton and a half and nobody could manage.

"What Shall We Do with the Skull of Nicephorus the First?" We know what happened to Nicephorus, but not to the skull-cup. Like many Byzantine emperors, he thought himself a better general than he was. He sacked the Bulgarian capital (Pliska) and treated the population with spectacular brutality (something of a tradition, later followed up by Basil II the Bulgar-slayer), but was then lured into the mountains, ambushed, and collected as a souvenir by the vengeful Bulgars.

"Hadrian's Tomb" was written after a visit to the Castel Sant'Angelo in Rome. Not much of the Roman building is left, though I found it a nice touch that someone had set up a plaque containing the emperor's famous poem to his soul in the niche where his ashes used to be. Opposite is the niche where the ashes of Septimius Severus used to reside. It is merely empty.

"In Ghostly Ravenna." The church of San Vitale, in Ravenna, is exquisite. Everyone has seen these mosaics reproduced in countless books, but it is quite another matter to see them for real. It was the first time I had ever seen Byzantine art in its proper context. The first impression is a blaze of color, which only later resolves into individual pictures. A beardless, late-Roman Christ floats above the altar. (My wife thought he looked like a Beatle. He has bangs.) The imperial mosaics are surprisingly small, perhaps six feet by three feet, but the figures in them seem to be ethereal, not entirely of this world, which was doubtless the artist's intention. The portrait of Justinian is from life, but it gazes out upon centuries.

"The Lost Dauphin Revisited." In reality the son of Louis XVI was imprisoned during the French Revolution and died a wretched death at about the age of ten. His heart was saved in a jar. Recently, DNA studies have determined that this is indeed the heart of a Bourbon. So much for all the survival tales. See Mark Twain's *Adventures of Huckleberry Finn* for a scoundrel trying to play this racket.

The poems in the last section turn toward science fiction. I have not been able to write much outright science fiction. Somehow my imagination does not work that way. But I have been able to make poems out of old science fiction imagery, like a collage artist rearranging scraps torn from magazines.

"Monsters of the Stratosphere" was suggested by "Through the Vortex" by Donald Keyhoe, published in *Weird Tales*, July 1926. Keyhoe later became a UFOlogist. You can see the beginnings of that in his fiction.

"The Steam-Man of the Prairies" was a character in a nineteenth-century dime novel. He seems a sadly comic caricature, but I decided he had a noble spirit inside. The image is widely reproduced in histories of science fiction, but I don't think anybody reads the novel.

"At the End of Time" of course evokes H. G. Wells's *The Time Machine.* I have since discovered that all those wonderfully resonant phrases that make the beginning and ending so memorable are not in the *Amazing Stories* printing of 1927, which follows an earlier, American edition. The text we know is that of the final revised version in *Seven Famous Novels of H. G. Wells* (1934).

"Where Have the Space Heroes Gone?" The heroes are Kimball Kinneson, the Gray Lensman, who figures largely in the Lensman series by Edward E. "Doc" Smith, Ph.D.; Captain Future, the hero of novels in a pulp magazine of the same title, most of them by Edmond Hamilton, the series recently revived by Allen Steele; John Carter of Mars, of course; Northwest Smith, a prototype of Han Solo, whose adventures on Mars and Venus were chronicled in *Weird Tales* in the 1930s by C. L. Moore; and Eric

John Stark, the hero of stories by Leigh Brackett published in *Planet Stories* in the 1940 and revived in a series of novels in the 1970s. My thanks are due to David Clink, who helped me get this poem in shape for its publication in the revived *Amazing*. It got me a Rhysling nomination, but, no, I did not win.

"Lacking an Adequate Metaphor for the Human Brain" is a response to an essay by Ted Chiang (science fiction writer, genius) published in *Lady Churchill's Rosebud Wristlet*.

"He Unwraps Himself" achieved my first and only appearance in the Datlow/Winding *Year's Best Fantasy and Horror* series. It is reprinted in the eighth volume in 1995. I have made the honorable mentions list many times, but this was my only appearance on the table of contents.

"The Skeptics." One reason this lost ancient Greek play remains lost is that it never existed. I made it up. The names are taken at random from Menander.

"Invocation." This only works if you pronounce it "He-KAT-ay," which I think is actually correct. Not "HECK-ate."

"Concerning the Fate of Philip, etc." Prester John (i.e., John the Priest), the mighty Christian king of Asia (or maybe Africa) was a potent medieval legend, probably based on garbled reports of some Nestorian Christian ruler in central Asia. For centuries, attempts were made to contact him and seek his aid against the Saracens. Never mind that he might have died of old age in the meantime! In the twelfth century an alleged letter *from* Prester John was received by the Pope, the German emperor, and the Byzantine emperor (Manuel Comnenus). The Pope's copy has survived. Nobody knows what happened to Philip. Robert Silverberg has written a good book on the subject, *The Realm of Prester John*.

"Signs and Portents." At Aquilea in the year 394, the army of the orthodox, Catholic, and legitimate Eastern emperor Theodosius the Great faced the pro-pagan, Western usurper Eugenius and his barbarian Master of Soldiers, Arbogastes. The Western army was the last in the history of the world to go into battle under the standards of Jupiter, with the blessing of the Olympian gods. Theodosius won. The results of this "experiment" were considered by contemporaries to be quite conclusive. This is arguably the moment at which the old gods died.

"The Sorcerer Contemplates His Beginnings" and the following poem were used to frame my 1995 novel, *The Mask of the Sorcerer*. Presumably, then, they were actually written by Sekenre the sorcerer and I only channeled them.

"Nuclear Spring." Lord Dunsany wrote a play (*The Use of Man*) in which the animals sit in judgment over mankind, but I was actually thinking of Chaucer's "The Parliament of Fowls." The bear seems to be quoting the Anglo-Saxon "Widsith." We English majors can pillage world literature like that.

"Cemetery Tour, Montreal, Early November 2001." This tour was given the evening after the World Fantasy Convention that year. We went to Montreal's most ancient cemetery, at dusk, on a rainy evening. It was as atmospheric as any fantasy or horror writer could have wanted, and yet, particularly when we came to the newer, underground vaults that were as clean and polished as shopping malls, with photographs of loved ones on the walls and candles flickering, I could not help but feel that we were intruding into something private, making light of someone else's still active grief. Centuries old spirits are used to this sort of thing, I am sure, but the recently dead are not.

"Those Who Do Not Find Their Way into Elfland." Ballad/folklore figures. Black Jack Davey was a Gypsy. Tam Lin was abducted by the fairies and had to be rescued by a lady. Tom O'Bedlam (who has a whole genre of "mad songs" devoted to him) was a lunatic. True Thomas sojourned in Elfland for many years and was given the "gift" of a tongue that could not lie. The last three lines are lifted from Lord Dunsany. See *The King of Elfland's Daughter*. No one ever put it better.

"A Barbaric Song." Discovered on a 20,000-year-old tablet of

Hyboria's Greatest Hits, this could well be a pop song from the era of Conan the Cimmerian. Or maybe not.

"I Think That We Are Witches Now." No, it wasn't a heart attack. It was hyperthyroidism. I actually collapsed at the airport on my way to a convention where I was to be, ironically, poetry guest of honor. Whether I have ever levitated in my pajamas or signed the Black Man's book, I refuse to divulge.

"A Further Voyage to Byzantium." Dare I write a reply to William Butler Yeats? We poets are an arrogant lot.

"They Sure Eat a Lot in Epics." A catastrophic beef barbecue is central episode of the *Odyssey*. I owe to Teresa Nielsen-Hayden the observation that epics were intended to be recited at kingly feasts and therefore were expected to give good food value.

"I Dreamed I Sailed in a Ship of Heroes." Autobiography again. The last time I saw my father alive, he was indeed in a hospital in Florida, where he had survived bypass surgery with flying colors and was cheerfully discussing with the doctor where he was going to park his car in two weeks when he came in for a checkup. So I flew home in good spirits. A blood clot killed him the next day.

"Remembering the Future." My most successful poem, at least financially. It earned me an extra $100 and a free breakfast when voted the best poem of the year by the readers of *Asimov's SF* in 2006. The bit about armed planets is from E. E. "Doc" Smith's *Second Stage Lensman* as quoted by Fritz Leiber in a chapter header in *The Wanderer*. Otherwise I've made the image resemble a series of Hubert Rogers covers from *Astounding*'s golden age. That future is behind us now, but it is still part of the central myth of science fiction.

ACKNOWLEDGMENTS

"*Amazing Stories* Covers" appears here for the first time.

"Angry in His Grave" first appeared in *Spectral Realms* No. 9 (Summer 2018).

"Artemidoros, Descendant of Croesus" first appeared in *Space and Time* No. 101 (Fall 2007).

"At the End of Time" first appeared in *Star*Line* (September–October 2007).

"Ballroom Dancing" first appeared in *Weird Fiction Review* No. 6 (Winter 2015).

"A Barbaric Song" first appeared in *The Cimmerian* (June 2006). Included in *Ghosts of Past and Future* (2008).

"Bold Voyager" first appeared in *Spectral Realms* No. 17 (Summer 2022).

"Cemetery Tour, Montreal, Early November 2001" first appeared in *Weird Tales* No. 336 (March 2004). Included in *Ghosts of Past and Future* (2008).

"The Colossi of Memnon Near Thebes" was first published in *Space and Time* No. 98 (Spring 2004). Included in *Ghosts of Past and Future* (2008).

"Dancing Before Azathoth" first appeared in *Spectral Realms* No. 14 (Winter 2021).

"Death Is the Great Unwinding" originally appeared in *The Book of Dark Wisdom* No. 7 (Fall 2005).

"Dreads" first appeared in *Weird Tales* No. 321 (Fall 2000). Included in *Ghosts of Past and Future* (2008).

"Drowning the Sacred Chickens" first appeared in *Paradox* No. 13 (Spring 2009).

"Each Evening Emily Dreamed of the Grave" first appeared in *Lore* No. 2 (Autumn 1995). Included in *Groping Toward the Light* (2000).

"Edgar Allan Poe Nears His End" first appeared in *Star*Line* (November/December 2004). Included in *Ghosts of Past and Future* (2008).

"Fairy Song" first appeared in *Spectral Realms* No. 1 (Summer 2014).

"A Further Voyage to Byzantium" first appeared in *Star*Line* (May/June 2003). Included in *Ghosts of Past and Future* (2008).

"The Ghosts of Troy" first appeared in *Talebones* No. 39 (Winter 2009).

"The Gods Do Not Pity Us" first appeared in *Journ-E* 1, No. 1 (Vernal Equinox 2022).

"Giants in the Earth" first appeared in *Spectral Realms* No. 18 (Winter 2023).

"Glastonbury, 1995" first appeared in *Mooreeffoc* (Fall 2001). Included in *Ghosts of Past and Future* (2008).

"The Gods We Left Behind" first appeared in *Mythic Delirium* No. 21 (Summer/Fall 2009).

"Grave-Robbing 2.0: Intermediate" first appeared in *Spectral Realms* No. 20 (Winter 2024).

"Hadrian's Tomb" first appeared in *Dreams and Nightmares* No. 88 (January 2011).

"He Unwraps Himself" first appeared in *Weird Tales* No. 306 (Spring 1994). Included in *Groping Toward the Light* (2000).

"Heretical Gospel" first appeared in *Crypt of Cthulhu* No. 105 (Lammas 2000). Included in *Groping Toward the Light* (2000).

"Homer Before the Trojan Court" first appeared in *Spectral Realms* No. 12 (Winter 2020).

"How Witches and Warlocks Do It" first appeared in *Journ-E* 1, No. 1 (Vernal Equinox 2022).

"The Howling House" first appeared in *Weird Fiction Review* No. 9 (Fall 2018).

"I Dreamed That I Sailed in a Ship of Heroes" first appeared in *Mooreeffoc* (Summer 2001). Included in *Ghosts of Past and Future* (2008).

"I Know There Are Giants under Our Hills" first appeared in *Penumbra* No. 3 (2022).

"I Think That We Are Witches Now" first appeared in *Star*Line* (November/December 2000). Included in *Ghosts of Past and Future* (2008).

"In Ghostly Ravenna" first appeared in *Dreams and Nightmares* No. 86 (May 2010).

"In the Ancient Lands" first appeared in *Dreams and Nightmares* No. 100 (January 2015).

"In the Roman Forum" first appeared in *Paradox* No. 11 (Autumn 2007).

"Invocation" first appeared in *Weird Tales* No. 298 (Fall 1990). Included in *Groping Toward the Light* (2000).

"Ithaca, Finally" first appeared in *Spectral Realms* No. 14 (Summer 2020).

"Lacking an Adequate Metaphor for the Human Brain" first appeared in *Andromeda Spaceways* No. 51 (2011).

"Lavinia Whateley" first appeared in *Spectral Realms* No. 2 (Winter 2015).

"Let Them Go" first appeared in *Isaac Asimov's Science Fiction Magazine* (November–December 2020).

"Look Beyond" first appeared in *Spectral Realms* No. 8 (Winter 2018).

"The Lost Dauphin Revisited 5, 2001" first appeared in *Mythic Delirium* (Summer/Fall 2001).

"The Mad Scientist's Assistant" first appeared in *Spectral Realms* No. 16 (Winter 2022).

"Malice Must Dwell within Your Heart" first appeared in *Spectral Realms* No. 7 (Summer 2022).

"Monsters of the Stratosphere" first appeared in *Isaac Asimov's Science Fiction Magazine* (April–May 2011).

"The Mysteries of the Worm" first appeared in *Penumbra* No. 1 (2020).

"Not All of Them Are Ghosts" first appeared in *Spectral Realms* No. 12 (Winter 2020).

"Not Your Typical Horror Poem" first appeared in *The Silver Web* (Winter/Spring 1993). Included in *Groping Toward the Light* (2000).

"Now We Are Joined" first appeared in *Weirdbook* No. 37 (Winter 2017).

"Nuclear Spring" first appeared in *Amazing Stories* (November 1989). Included in *Groping Toward the Light* (2000).

"Odysseus in the Underworld for the Second Time" first appeared in *Space and Time* No. 134 (Autumn 2019).

"Odysseus May Have Been a Scoundrel" first appeared in *Spectral Realms* No. 14 (Winter 2021).

"The Old Retainer's Tale" first appeared in *Mythic Delirium* No. 7 (Summer/Fall 2002).

"Only in Dreams" first appeared in *Spectral Realms* No. 5 (Summer 2016).

"Only the Trees and Stones Remember" first appeared in *Journ-E* 2, No. 1 (20 March 2023).

"Our Ghosts Are Going Away" first appeared in *Spectral Realms* No. 15 (Summer 2021).

"Patiently Waiting" originally appeared in *Weird Tales* No. 335 (March/April 2004).

"Penelope, Sleepless" first appeared in *Weirdbook* No. 32 (2016).

"The Poetry of Evil Must Never Be Shouted" first appeared in *Spectral Realms* No. 4 (Winter 2016).

"The Promise" first appeared in *Spectral Realms* No. 2 (Winter 2015).

"Remembering the Future" first appeared in *Isaac Asimov's Science Fiction Magazine* (October/November 2006). Included in *Ghosts of Past and Future* (2008).

"Romance" first appeared in *Skelos* No. 4 (Fall 2020).

"Scientific Romance" first appeared in *Star*Line* (November/December 2005). Included in *Ghosts of Past and Future* (2008).

"The Secret Pool" first appeared in *Spectral Realms* No. 11 (Summer 2019).

"Signs and Portents" first appeared *Groping Toward the Light* (Wildside Press, 2000).

"Sir Boss Remembered" first appeared in *Star*Line* (November/December 2001). Included in *Ghosts of Past and Future* (2008).

"The Skeptics" first appeared in *Star*Line* (September–October 1999). Included in *Groping Toward the Light* (2000).

"Some Books Are Forbidden for Good Reason" first appeared in *Spectral Realms* No. 20 (Winter 2024).

"The Sorcerer Contemplates His Beginnings" first appeared *Weird Tales* No. 303 (Winter 1991/92). Included in *Groping Toward the Light* (2000).

"The Sorcerer in His Tower Contemplating Possible Success" first appeared in *Spectral Realms* No. 19 (Summer 2023).

"The Sorcerer to His Long-Lost Love" first appeared in *Eldritch Tales* No. 21 (Fall 1989). Included in *Groping Toward the Light* (2000).

"Sparta, in Decline" first appeared in *Paradox* No. 12 (Spring 2008).

"Specter, You Have Nothing to Say to Me" first appeared in *Weird Fiction Review* No. 2 (Fall 2011).

"The Steam-Man of the Prairies" first appeared in *Andromeda Spaceways* No. 60 (May 2014).

"10 Reasons Not to Write a List Poem" first appeared in *Mythic Delirium* No. 17 (Summer/Fall 2007).

"They Believed in Fairies During World War I" first appeared in *Isaac Asimov's Science Fiction Magazine* (February 2009).

"They Sure Eat a Lot in Epics" first appeared in *Lady Churchill's Rosebud Wristlet* No. 9 (November 2001). Included in *Ghosts of Past and Future* (2008).

"The Thing in the Box" first appeared in *Weird Fiction Review* No. 8 (Fall 2017).

"Those That We Meet in Dark Country Lanes" first appeared in *Spectral Realms* No. 16 (Winter 2022).

"Those Who Do Not Find Their Way into Elfland" first appeared in *Talebones* No. 25 (Fall 2002). Included in *Ghosts of Past and Future* (2008).

"Tourists from Outer Space" first appeared in *Isaac Asimov's Science Fiction Magazine* (October–November 2010).

"Two Knights" first appeared *The Weirdbook Sampler* No. 3 (1988). Included in *Groping Toward the Light* (2000).

"Very Long Conversations Between the Stars" first appeared in *Andromeda Spaceways* No. 49 (2010).

"We Who Have Encountered Monsters" first appeared in *Spectral Realms* No. 14 (Winter 2016).

"Werewolf Poem" appears here for the first time.

"What If I Were Secretly the Phoenix?" *Mythic Delirium* No. 20 (Winter/Spring 2009)

"What Shall We Do with the Skull of Nicephorus the First?" first appeared in *Alexiad* 5, No. 1 (February 2006).

"When Time Travelers from the Future Finally Reach Us" first appeared in *Isaac Asimov's Science Fiction Magazine* (March–April 2018).

"Where Have the Space Heroes Gone?" first appeared in *Amazing Stories* 71, No. 1 (Fall 2019).

"Which Remained Untold" first appeared in *Weirdbook* No. 34 (2017).

"Witches in Winter" first appeared in *Ghosts of Past and Future* (Wildside Press, 2008).

"Word Salad" appears here for the first time.

"The World's Ending Again in 2012" first appeared in *Isaac Asimov's Science Fiction Magazine* (December 2009).

www.ingramcontent.com/pod-product-compliance
Lightning Source LLC
Chambersburg PA
CBHW051842090426
42736CB00011B/1922